THE NEW
REFORMERS

THE NEW REFORMERS

Forces for Change in American Politics

STEPHEN C. SCHLESINGER

Houghton Mifflin Company Boston   1975

Library of Congress Cataloging in Publication Data
Schlesinger, Stephen.
The new reformers.
Includes bibliographical references and index.
1. Political parties—United States. 2. United
States—Politics and government—1945–   3. Social
reformers—United States. I. Title.
JK2263 1975.S33   322.4′0973   75–9943
ISBN 0–395–20709–6
ISBN 0–395–21597–8 pbk.

Printed in the United States of America

w 10 9 8 7 6 5 4 3 2 1

To My Mother and Father

"The history of reform is always identical,
it is the comparison of the idea with the fact."

—RALPH WALDO EMERSON

Acknowledgments

I COULD NOT have written a detailed study of the contemporary reform movements without the help of all the individuals who aided in the reformer's magazine, *The New Democrat*. I would like to express my deepest appreciation to the following people, whose unselfish devotion of time and generous contribution of support kept *The New Democrat* alive from April 1970 to July 1972: Grier Raggio, Dorothy Plohn, Eleanor Jackson, Laurie Lazar, John Hickman, Timothy Collins, Mike Kramer, Mrs. Gardner Cox, Jeff Cowan, Mike Duberstein, Dick Conlon, Rick Meyerowitz, Peter Darrow, Day Patterson, Stephen Smith, Ramsey Clark, Howard Samuels, Judy Gordon, John Roberts, Ken Bode, Bill Samuels, Verne Newton, Robert Trentlyon, Stewart Mott, John Kenneth Galbraith, Susan MacKenzie, Blair Clark, Allen Weinstein, Jack Newfield, Joseph Rauh, Jr., Michael Hudner, James Hightower, Stephen Kinzer, Ted Van Dyk, Kirby Jones, Page Cole, Jeff Greenfield, Harvey Sloane, Merrie Spaeth, Rich Cohen, Ron Aigen, John Boni, Malcolm Frouman, Abe Hirschfeld, Ed Cohen, Timothy Cooney, my grandmother Mrs. Arthur M. Schlesinger, Sr., all the unpaid contributors of articles, all the correspondents of the magazine across the country, and finally the subscribers.

I wish to thank also the many persons in the reform movements who kindly consented to be interviewed for this book: Alan Baron, Representative William Steiger (R–Wisconsin), Bobbie Greene Kilberg, Representative Bella Abzug (D–New York), Doris Meissner, Brenda Feigen Fasteau, Frances Farenthold, Frank Mankiewicz, Jeff Smith, Jane McMichael, Robert Maynard, Augustus A. Adair, Jerry Wurf, Michael Harrington, Bill Lucy, Floyd Smith, Victor Gotbaum, Joseph Beirne, Joseph Rauh, Jr., David Selden, Mildred Jeffrey, Msgr. George Higgens, Bernard Sorokin, Linda Davidoff, Sarah Kovner, Dan Collins, Richard Wade, Arnold Weiss, Richard Conlon, Representative James O'Hara (D–Michigan), Representative Donald Fraser (D–Minnesota), Representative Phillip Burton (D–California), David Broder, Representative Thomas P. ("Tip") O'Neill, Jr. (D–Massachusetts), Representative Richard Bolling (D–Missouri), and Herbert Alexander.

I want finally to acknowledge my deep gratitude for those special friends who, when my spirits flagged, gave me their unselfish support, and when my manuscript most needed revision, generously contributed frank criticisms and useful suggestions to me: George Crile III, Andrea Marsh, Stephen Kinzer, Wendy Weil, and my parents.

Lastly an expression of profound thanks to my editor, Joyce Hartman, who labored so carefully over the text of the book and to whom should go most of the credit for any style and coherence this study exhibits.

Although I am appreciative of the people who backed me up, I must emphasize that the responsibility for all errors or mistakes as well as facts and conclusions in this book is solely my own.

Stephen C. Schlesinger

Contents

Introduction

A MOVEMENT for social reform in America exists today without a leader and without a party. It consists of almost a dozen loosely allied political groups made up of party reformers, women, blacks, liberal unions, white middle-class liberals, progressives in Congress, and the newly aroused minorities: Chicanos (Mexican-Americans), Puerto Ricans, Indians, and Gays.

I call them "the new reformers," but they are also variously known as "the radical-liberals," "the left-liberals," "the New Left," "the New Politics," "the New Populists," or "the progressives." They are "reformers" in the sense that they believe fundamental political change can be achieved within the accepted legal constraints set out by the Constitution of the United States, through the contemporary party structures, and by dint of the vision and intelligence of present-day political leaders.

They are contemporary echoes of the old progressives of the early twentieth century and the New Deal reformers of the thirties. Like their illustrious predecessors, the modern reformers believe in enlarging the economic opportunities for neglected minorities in the United States. They advocate greater freedom for individuals to pursue their own social beliefs. They propose a more equitable distribution of wealth and resources in the country.

While the current new reformers are motivated by particular ideals (women's rights and racial equality, among others), they have together demonstrated an acute appreciation of the exercise of political power for one broad purpose. They managed once to nominate a presidential candidate — George McGovern in 1972. They kept alive the drive to open up and reform the tottering structures of the two parties so that both parties have increasing participation from women and minorities. They are the groups who habitually raise fresh issues and tackle the controversies that most leaders in the parties avoid.

The new reformers have also shown that they accurately reflect social change in the country. The women reformers are part of the widespread movement among women to gain equal rights in society. The evolution of the blacks into a major political force is the result of a long decade of civil rights agitation in the sixties. The emergence of a functioning party reform movement is a consequence of the prolonged and well-organized antiwar activity during the last two presidential election campaigns.

These individual reform movements, though, have not replaced the more established reform organizations in the country. For example, the National Committee for an Effective Congress (NCEC) and the more centrist Committee on Political Education (COPE) of the AFL-CIO regularly distribute large sums of money to progressive or prolabor candidates. The Americans for Democratic Action (ADA) is still influential in shaping new issues.

These new caucuses have actually, in some ways, become the precinct workers for the older progressive lobbies, which (except for COPE) have largely eschewed direct political action. The reform caucuses are truly products of the contemporary age — nurtured by civil rights marches, antiwar demonstrations, and the TV news. Most of them hold conventions, make endorsements, attempt to disseminate their ideas, train political workers, interview candidates, raise money, exert pressure on legislators, picket and heckle the opposition, swell up in election years and shrink in nonelection years, and generate vocal, energetic, and passionate activists.

The coalition-building potential of the new reformers, however, is uncertain. What the new reformers have always sought is an elusive coalition of progressives, centrists, and conservatives formed around a candidate who can stir up the voters' emotions on issues of change — as Roosevelt did in 1932 and Kennedy in 1960. But the McGovern loss in 1972 has shown that elements within the new movements chronically resist the lessons of the past, either by refusing to establish alliances with more moderate groups in order to win elections, or making separate deals with regular politicians at the expense of a reform coalition as a whole. Furthermore, the movements lack a coherent reform vision. Since these organizations all were initially aroused by a single cause, they are, except on certain large issues like the Vietnam War, as yet unaccustomed to fighting for broader political agenda. Movements of reformers uninformed by larger common goals are doomed to waste their resources on irrelevant internal disputes and to dissipate their energies on fruitless external crusades. These perils threaten today's new reformers.

Lastly, the new reformers have not proven yet that they can affect the feelings of many American voters. The reformers have, in large measure, failed in recent years to convince the ethnic groups, blue-collar workers, and many old-style party members that they have more in common with poor black youths, welfare mothers, and the unemployed than with the corporate giants and the stockbrokers. The reformers also have not demonstrated to them that high taxes, crime, drug abuse, poor schools, and inflation can be solved with reform programs and will not be solved with conservative rhetoric — because the problems require an attack on basic causes, not on symptoms.

The new reformers have thus made themselves vulnerable to fusillades by conservative theorists like Richard Scammon and Ben Wattenberg, whose book, *The Real Majority*, excoriates the reform movements as repugnant to lower- and middle-class values; and to the "new conservative" intellectuals like Irving Kristol and Norman Podhoretz, who dismiss the appeals to new constituencies as "shrill" and "elitist" and "unrepresentative of the masses."

The new reformers are today attempting to confront their weaknesses in order to take political power. They are looking for ways to reconstruct the old progressive and liberal coalitions of the past and to revive their appeal to broad constituencies. They want to transform what made possible the short-lived triumph of McGovern's nomination into what makes possible American politics in both parties in the future. This book is an attempt to explore some of the directions that reformers must take next if they are to influence American politics decisively in the coming decade.

First of all, it is evident the new reformers cannot successfully bid for power in either party without understanding how party structures have changed. Drastic alterations have already been made by both parties in the process by which delegates are selected, in the formation of the national conventions, in the distribution of political authority. In addition, reformers in 1976 will not enjoy the same head start the rules changes gave them at the 1972 Democratic Convention. In the future, conservative candidates and organizations will be just as adept as were the reformers at utilizing the delegate guidelines. The opening chapter analyzes the impact of the party changes on the new reformers in both the Republican and Democratic parties.

Secondly, the new reformers are not going to be able to lay the foundations for a succesful political movement until they can cope fully with the problems and strengths of their own caucuses. Chapters 2 through 7 explain in detail the developments of the major reform movements since their emergence around 1968. These are the most influential of the reform cadres and their principal organizations: women — the National Women's Political Caucus; blacks — the Congressional Black Caucus; labor — the coalition of progressive unions; middle-class white liberals — the New Democratic Coalitions; Congress — the Democratic Study Group in the House; minorities — the movements of the Chicanos, the Puerto Ricans, the Indians, and the Gays.

Finally, the new reformers must face the most important issue of all — building a majority coalition for the coming years. Such a coalition, which must include centrists and conservatives, may be able to take power in 1976 — but only if the reformers produce an attractive candidate who can expound the issues that motivate and excite the blue-collar workers and the white middle class as well as the minorities. The concluding chapter addresses itself to the shaping of that coalition.

The book does not include an account of the political reform efforts among the Jews, the Italians, the aged, the students, and other interest groups. All of them have traditional liberal lobbies, but none has yet, in my view, developed a significant party reform organization in the United States, although some, like the aged, are on the verge of establishing an effective voter's caucus, perhaps by 1976.

The book also does not discuss the traditional liberal organizations like the ADA, or public-interest organizations such as Ralph Nader's Public Citizen or John Gardner's Common Cause. These associations have tangential resemblances to the six reform movements discussed here: they have all emerged as vital forces in the past decade or earlier, have advanced progressive ideas, and have large followings. But, except for the ADA, none have nominated and run candidates for political office, or made political alliances with other groups to achieve electoral influence, or directly sought power in either major party, and all are obligated to remain unaligned politically by their founding charters.

This book, in brief, describes the new political reform movements, explores their role in the current decade of American politics, and explains where they are likely to be going in future years.

THE NEW
REFORMERS

1 ☆

The Parties Reform

A CHANGE in political rules was the most powerful stimulant to the emergence of the new reformers in the United States. The Democratic Party adopted the changes in the riotous 1968 convention. The new guidelines encouraged the participation in politics by bodies of voters — the women, the blacks, the antiwar forces, the middle-class liberals, the minorities — who had been shattered by the Chicago disorders and Nixon's victory in 1968, and who were, for a time, unrepresented, unconsulted, and ill-regarded by the political leaders in both parties.

It was an odd mix of pluck and luck that led to these alterations in the Democratic Party's constitution. The original resolution to set up two commissions on party reforms (the so-called McGovernor-Fraser Commission on Party Structure and Delegate Selection, and the O'Hara Commission on Rules) passed the 1968 Democratic Convention almost incidentally, as a sop to the rebellious legions of Kennedy and McCarthy supporters who believed that Lyndon Johnson and the party organization had manipulated the old rules to fix the nomination for Hubert Humphrey.

The dissidents, in general, knew whereof they spoke. In the

1

bad old days of 1968, state party leaders, in many cases, arbitrarily selected delegations with little reference to the sentiments of Democratic voters, even though by 1967 and 1968 many Democrats were against the war. Governor Lester Maddox of Georgia, for instance, the scrappy, racist, ax-wielding restaurant owner, stamped his views on his state delegation by using his power as governor to appoint every one of its members. The leader of the United Steelworkers of America, I. W. Abel, with his enormous influence in Pennsylvania, helped arrange for 80 percent of Pennsylvania's delegates to go to Hubert Humphrey, even though a Pennsylvania primary result showed that 83 percent of the voters favored Robert Kennedy or Eugene McCarthy. Missouri's party machine locked out the liberals. Michigan's precinct chairmen, elected two years earlier in 1966 — before McCarthy and Kennedy and the Tet offensive — chose that state delegation.[1] Long outraged by these accumulated inequities, the reformers demanded changes at the 1968 convention; the Humphrey-Johnson contingents, hoping to win the reformers back for the election, did not vehemently oppose the resolution and it passed.

The crucial words, as adopted in the majority report of the Credentials Committee (voted by the convention on August 28, 1968), provided that: "We can and should encourage appropriate revisions in the delegate selection processes to assure the fullest possible participation and to make the Democratic Party completely representative of grass roots sentiment." The resolution also created the party's two special commissions to define and implement this broad mandate.

In 1969, the Democratic National Committee set up the most controversial of these commissions — the Party Structure and Delegate Selection Commission — under the chairmanship of Senator George McGovern. It began to hold a series of hearings around the country, which few party regulars attended. Ultimately, the McGovern Commission came up with eighteen "guidelines," which set stiff standards for fair delegate selection, abolished proxy voting and the unit rule (though allowing the winner-take-all in some states), required that delegate selection take place within the calendar year of the convention, and directed states with convention systems to choose at least 75 percent of their delegations on congressional district levels or on smaller units — thereby better assuring representation for minority blocs. But the most critical guidelines were A-1 and A-2, which mandated that state primaries, within a full, meaningful, and timely period, "overcome the effects of past discrimination by affirmative steps to encourage representation on the National Convention delegation of minority groups, young people and women in reasonable relationship to their presence in the population in the state."[2] The antiwar activists and civil rights adherents, who had fared badly in the 1968 debacle, insisted on inserting this specific language because, although previous conventions had also outlawed and deplored this sort of discrimination, they had practiced it all the same.

My own interest in the reforms developed as the guidelines were being drawn up and applied. During 1969 and 1970, however, I was more troubled by an aridity of spirit which seemed to me to be making a desert out of the Democratic Party. The leaders of the party had somehow interpreted the 1968 explosion in Chicago as a sign to eliminate all dissidence, rather than to open up Democratic politics to the high-spirited, sometimes raucous, but richly innovative, legions of 1968.

Indeed, with seeming premeditation after Chicago, the party's *apparatchiks* had lowered the Democrats' voice to a mumble and had, themselves, avoided speaking publicly of the rebels. Senate Majority Leader Mike Mansfield and House Speaker John McCormack (and, later, Carl Albert) handled party leadership like workers punching time clocks — in a mechanical and automatic way — and made no mention of issues. Democratic National Chairman Lawrence O'Brien rebuffed attempts to institute a reform-minded policy group to draw up new programs for the Democrats, even though he sanctioned the creation of an innocuous advisory group that issued vapid pronouncements from time to time.

Increasingly distressed by what, with others, I regarded as this senseless withdrawal by the Democrats, in mid-1969 I left my job in a New York state urban renewal program. In consulting with many former Kennedy-McCarthy organizers, I discovered they shared with me the same fear: that unless we acted now to organize, demand our influence, and claim our rights as Democratic reformers, the opportunity would never again arise to return the party to its original humanitarian ideals and to end the exclusion we had suffered in Chicago.

After many discussions about the possibility of creating a liberal bloc or a reform forum or some kind of new politics opposition within the party, a number of us decided to set up a political journal for progressive ideas within the party. The project was somewhat akin to *The Ripon Forum*, a monthly magazine that a band of liberal-minded young Republicans had established in 1962 to counter the know-nothingism of Goldwater and to set their party on a more progressive course.

Publication of our new magazine soon began to resemble a political crusade. We visited wealthy contributors to plead for funds; sought out intellectuals, politicians, writers, editors for

4

counsel and aid; saw printers, mailers, postal officials, advertisers. The effort at first seemed in vain. But by the beginning of 1970, after a few successful mailings and some generous individual donations, we had acquired a staff, office space in New York City, some "seed" money, and a quickening sense of mission.

My partner in the enterprise was a college classmate, Grier Raggio from Texas, a transplanted Southern populist practicing law in New York at the time. A young woman, Dorothy Plohn from Nebraska, joined the staff as an assistant editor and became one of the small band of workers who kept the magazine alive despite a poverty wage of fifty dollars a week paid irregularly. Later, two other young women, Laurie Lazar and Eleanor Jackson, came in to help edit and stayed on in spite of our dismal financial condition. Finally, John Roberts, who had conceived and funded the famous Woodstock Festival in upstate New York in 1969, took pity on us when we were unable to find free office space, and gave us several empty rooms in his suite in Manhattan, rent free.

We decided to name the magazine *The New Democrat* in an attempt to broadcast immediately to foes and friends that we aimed to be a voice for new impulses in the party. We announced rather grandiloquently that *The New Democrat* was "published with the intention of stimulating fresh thinking in the Democratic Party. It will provide individuals with a platform to enunciate ideas, with an arena to voice discontents, and with a bullhorn to attack old politics." We set publication monthly. We had no idea at that time that we would last almost two and a half years, finally suspending publication in July 1972, when George McGovern was nominated.

Our first issue came out in April 1970, and we concentrated

5

our analysis principally on the weaknesses of party spokesmen, the dearth of ideas in the party, and the pusillanimity of our national leaders in the face of the burning issues of the day — Vietnam, Cambodia, busing. Much to our surprise, as the monthly issues began to roll out, *The New Democrat* gained both favor and a certain notoriety. Progressives started to applaud and write letters; conservative columnists from as far away as the Dallas *News* denounced us; and money — not enough but some — began to come in.

What eventually gave us our shape and character, however, was the issue of reform in the Democratic Party. None of those on our tiny staff was at first aware of the magnitude of the reform enterprise. But we slowly became conscious that something dramatic was happening in the country. Complaints began to trickle into our office from reformers who decried the laxity and hostility of officials in applying the McGovern-Fraser Commission guidelines to local parties. Friends on the various reform commissions in Washington, including the Commission on Rules headed by Congressman James O'Hara from Michigan (which apportioned delegates and review procedures for the convention), began to warn us that obstructionism by party regulars was impeding both the McGovern Commission and O'Hara Commission recommendations.

Since no other magazine or newspaper was keeping a close tab on the national reforms, we started to concentrate more and more on the reform fight. Our investigative reporter, Verne Newton, a young political activist, went regularly to Washington to check out allegations about the sabotage of the reform process. We began to print articles on the changes, including pieces by McGovern, the original head of the Commission on Party Structure and Delegate Selection; his chief counsel, Eli Segal; and his research director, Dr. Kenneth Bode. We also ran commentaries by blacks, women, and young people on the impact of the reforms on their constituencies; and we ran indignant protests by reformers in such states as Missouri, Tennessee, Delaware, and others against the wretched condition of compliance in their areas.

The New Democrat criticized party chairman Lawrence O'Brien for his resistance to the reforms. O'Brien gave the impression — whether intentionally or not — of a man who was going about the business of modifying or diluting the reforms according to some Holy guidance, to which he alone had access. One tactic he used often was the threat to set up his own ad hoc committee to "implement" the guidelines. We considered this to be a ruse behind which he planned to ax the McGovern changes; in other petty ways he also obstructed, delayed, and harassed the reformers. Our drumbeat of criticism, in all fairness, never disturbed his outward serenity, though he complained bitterly about us in private. He was too shrewd a tactician to give us publicity by instigating a public row.

At last, out of an acute sense of futility, we ran an editorial in November 1971 headlined, "It's Time To Go, Larry." We demanded his resignation for "systematically" weakening the guidelines on minorities and reopening the old wounds in the party by his hostility toward the reformers. O'Brien for the first and only time replied to us — through his press spokesman. O'Brien's factotum snapped: "Mr. O'Brien has a reform record that nobody can top." Ironically, that was the month when O'Brien finally capitulated to the women's movement and agreed that 50 percent of all delegations should consist of

7

women or be subject to challenge. By 1972, O'Brien had, to his credit, turned fully around on the reforms, but his conversion was grudging and late. McGovern, after his nomination, removed him as national chairman and appointed in his place a woman, Jean Westwood from Utah.

In other quarters, our criticisms were muffled by a thick wall of silence. The national press seemed but dimly aware of the extent of the party changes and therefore gave only passing coverage to the commissions. Party officials downgraded the reforms. Many intelligent and sophisticated Democrats, including just about all the presidential candidates (with, of course, one notable exception — the commission chairman) were simply unaware of what was going on. We began to feel we were shouting in a political world inhabited by the deaf and dumb.

Fortunately, the pressure on the Democratic Party from other sectors was unrelenting. One of the most influential among the critics was Dr. Kenneth Bode. In 1970, he left the McGovern-Fraser Commission and set up the Center For Political Reform to monitor the progress of the reforms. His industriousness, his intimate knowledge of the guidelines, and his unflagging energy enabled him to demolish the arguments of those in the party who opposed any changes at all. Day after day, he exerted pressure for compliance on the Democratic state parties with a blizzard of lawsuits, press releases, articles in *The New Republic* and *The New Democrat*, public testimony, and frequent visits to individual states. He supported the demands of all the minority movements and helped them gain representation.

Gradually, the constituencies to which the reforms were addressed — the women, blacks, labor, middle-class white lib-

The Parties Reform

erals, Chicanos — began to respond and organize politically. A
Jacksonian type of upheaval appeared to be in the making. The
minorities skillfully exploited the guidelines, particularly the
ambiguous A-1 and A-2. A-1 and A-2 didn't make clear how
the principle of minority representation was to be realized;
many of the reform caucuses consequently began to press for
quotas. They did so in some cases because they were new to
politics and edgy about their rights, and in other cases because
there were no affirmative-action programs in which they could
participate and gain delegate slots.

In November 1971, Congressman Donald Fraser (D–
Minnesota), who succeeded Senator McGovern as chairman
of the Commission on Party Structure and Delegate Selection,
wrote a letter to the state parties at Chairman O'Brien's request, saying that they "should be on notice that whenever
the proportion of women, minorities and young people . . .
is less than the proportion of these groups in the total population . . . a challenge will constitute a prima facie showing of
violation of the guidelines."[3] Some of the new groups then
managed to bluff state organizations into interpreting the
"population" standard as a demographic quota, though
Fraser's letter only recommended an honest effort by the
states to meet the population criteria. Harried presidential
candidates, nervous about possible credentials challenges or
about appearing unsympathetic toward certain groups of
voters, began to comply strictly with the census bureau figures.

The population standards may have provided precise quotas,
but they could readily be abused. Candidates could employ
the demographic profiles to manipulate minorities for ideological ends and vice versa; the standards themselves were of
dubious worth in an assemblage that was convened solely to

9

reflect political views; and, in any event, the standards limited the representation of groups arbitrarily, omitting, say, black Americans, Italo-Americans, Jewish Americans, the aged, the poor, and other minorities. Therefore, the use of quotas was not defensible as a permanent practice. It did, however, bring about a rather astounding tumbling down of the walls that for so long had blocked many groups from effective representation at the Democratic Convention.

The New Democrat was watching these new movements from a special and intimate vantage point. Because of the nature of the magazine's ideological predilections and its stated desire to assist the new movements in gaining delegates, the journal's staff was in touch almost daily with the reform organizations throughout the country.

The blacks very quickly understood the importance of the reforms. In 1968, they cast about 20 percent of the Democratic vote though they constituted only 5.5 percent of the delegates. This serious under-representation led them, by 1972, under the leadership of the Congressional Black Caucus in the House of Representatives and of freshly elected black officials, to launch a three-pronged strategy to elect black delegates — behind the presidential candidacy of Representative Shirley Chisholm, through unaffiliated blocs, and through the delegations of other candidates.

Then the Spanish-speaking Americans, specifically the Chicanos and Puerto Ricans, shamefully neglected in the political process because of linguistic and cultural differences, also began to awaken to the significance of the reforms. The Chicanos were strong in the Southwest; the Puerto Ricans in the Northeast. Even the Indians, long distrustful of white society, began to enter local delegation contests. Another minority, the homosexuals, also took to the hustings in certain large cities in pursuit of representation at the 1972 Democratic Convention.

In due course, middle-class white liberals — "good government" advocates, students, suburbanites, intellectuals — all of them constituting a traditional progressive force in the Democratic Party, became heavily involved in lobbying for the reforms throughout fifty states. They created statewide caucuses called the New Democratic Coalitions (NDCs). The local NDCs used the party guidelines to elect delegates for the reform candidate, Senator McGovern. They also worked for the selection of more young delegates through such organizations as the National Youth Caucus.

The progressive labor unions, a small but growing force, including a few AFL-CIO unions and several independent unions outside the federation, also saw in the guidelines a means to elect delegates. Though, after the 1968 election, George Meany's domination of the AFL-CIO had turned most of labor against the party reforms, a few unions, including the United Auto Workers and the Communications Workers of America (who supported Humphrey in 1968 but later split with Meany), showed up at the McGovern hearings to endorse delegate changes. The progressive unions took most of the labor delegates to the 1972 convention.

Perhaps those most active — and most influential — in using the guidelines were the women. They were the only "minority" that was not a minority. In 1972, they actually represented about 53 percent of the voting population. Their movement grew slowly over the sixties, through organizations like NOW (National Organization for Women), which took on the legal battles to enforce women's equality as the

NAACP had done for blacks in the fifties. Then the women's crusade exploded politically in 1971 with the creation of the National Women's Political Caucus (NWPC).

The NWPC conceived of itself as the political arm of NOW and other feminist groups, devoted, in a bipartisan coalition, to the election of both Democratic and Republican women. Its prime strategist was the fiery Democratic representative from New York, Bella Abzug. She immediately persuaded the Democratic progressives in the NWPC (who were perhaps 80 percent of the group) to work on reform guidelines in the Democratic Party. This quickly led to the formation of the group called Women's Education for Delegate Selection (WEDS), which sent emissaries to the states to encourage women to run for delegate slots and to put pressure on candidates and state parties to assure at least 50 percent representation by women on all delegations.

Another subsidiary but very powerful bloc of reformers was the informal alliance of progressives in the House of Representatives, the Democratic Study Group (DSG). The House reformers had the majority of the members of the Democratic Party, the majority party in Congress — but majorities meant little when the committee chairmen claimed the power of life and death over legislation. The progress of the national party reforms spurred the DSG in its crusade to restructure the House. A reform within a reform took place.

Many who thought themselves quite sophisticated in the byways of reform politics were unprepared for the vast dimensions of the changes. In particular, the composition of delegates at the Democratic Convention showed how extraordinary a revolution had occurred: women shot up from 13 percent in 1968 to 40 percent in 1972; blacks from 5.5 percent to 15 percent; young people from 4 percent to 21 percent; Latinos more than quadrupled, from 1 percent to 4.5 percent; labor members increased significantly to 16 percent.

Reflecting several years later on these events, I was struck by how swiftly the reform groups had been able to utilize the guidelines to capture delegates. It seemed to me that this was the result of skill and luck. First, the reformers were taking no chances in 1972, after all the indignities they had suffered in Chicago in 1968. While conservatives and party regulars dozed, they followed Pascal's old axiom that "chance comes to the prepared mind," and, quietly and unnoticed, they capitalized on the reforms.

Second, a suddenly fashionable fealty to the guidelines developed in 1972 because of the highly sensitive atmosphere of the primary contests, in which no candidates could afford to lose votes or face challenges on their tickets by disregarding the new constituencies. This placed on all the other presidential contenders a burden that might not have otherwise existed: namely, "balancing their slates."

Third, party regulars, still bloated from their success at the 1968 convention, lapsed into an unusual apathy, believing that all the ancient tricks for winning nominations would still work. Their strategy consisted of endorsements, inflated promises, media rather than grass-roots campaigns, optimistic delegate estimates, and basic neglect of the reforms until it was too late.

Finally, reform was one of those egalitarian ideas whose moment had apparently arrived. Like the Jacksonian upheaval of the 1820s, or the passage of the Nineteenth Amendment in 1920 giving women the vote, or the Twenty-sixth

13

Amendment in 1971 giving people of eighteen or older the right to cast a ballot, the time was ripe in 1972 to enfranchise the neglected minorities.

After the election and McGovern's defeat, however, the reforms were in trouble. Cries for retribution were heard from many segments of the party. For many, it was an unnerving replay of the post-Chicago period in 1968. George Meany lambasted McGovern and began to retaliate against reformers on the Democratic National Committee through COPE. Supporters of Senator Henry Jackson formed a conservative organization called the Coalition for a Democratic Majority (CDM) to scuttle the reforms. Leaders of white ethnic groups, of the poor, the party regulars, all complained bitterly that the reforms had underrepresented them at the convention. Liberal critics, like Jack Newfield of *The Village Voice*, accurately noted that "the McGovern reform guidelines created quotas for women, youths and blacks but none for poor people, or senior citizens or ethnic minorities — Irish, Italian, Polish . . ."[4] Difficult questions arose over what constituted a "balanced" delegation: does a woman of Hungarian descent married to a Greek qualify as a white ethnic or a Greek or a female or something else? George McGovern himself soon favored modifying the party guidelines his own commission had produced.

It was a profoundly troubling moment. The reforms did undoubtedly awaken the political consciousness of long disregarded minorities in the Democratic Party and proved to be extraordinarily useful in expanding participation in 1972. But it was dismaying that other voting blocs, particularly the European ethnics, who were traditional Democratic supporters, had not been well served by the changes. Now, in addition, the regulars recaptured the national committee through the conservative national chairman, Robert Strauss. This appeared to be a signal that all the reforms would be totally scrapped, ending any chance for keeping the party open.

But in 1973 and 1974, something unusual took place. Barbara Mikulski, an "inner city" councillor from Baltimore who was the new head of the Reform Commission, led a fierce goal-line stand against the attacks on the guidelines. By the end of 1973, her commission produced new rules, which retained the basic guidelines; in mid-1974, the Democratic National Committee approved them, and, at the close of 1974, the Democratic Party's first midterm convention overwhelmingly incorporated the rules — with minor changes — in the party's new charter.

Most reform advocates were relieved, for the revamped rules, in effect, put a greater burden on the state parties to set up strong affirmative-action programs for insuring, in the words of the new guidelines, representation of "all Democrats with particular concern for minority groups, Native Americans, women and youth . . ." ("all Democrats" was added to take in the white ethnics, the party regulars, and other constituencies who had been poorly represented at the 1972 convention[5]). The new guidelines, which also categorically eliminated any use of quotas, most significantly contained another historic change in the party rules mandated by the 1972 convention — the adoption of a semiproportional representation system to guarantee attendance for the smallest minorities.

The new system ended entirely the winner-take-all results in caucus or convention states and in those primary states in which voters balloted for presidential candidates or slates of delegates (although a de facto winner-take-all arrangement still exists on a congressional-district basis in certain states and could actually reduce the number of 1976 delegates selected by proportional representation to less than 50 percent of the total). No longer would the historic situation be possible in which 51 percent of the vote gave a candidate 100 percent of the delegates. Now, any candidate or slate that commanded 15 percent or above of the vote had to have that backing accounted for in delegates at every stage of the delegate-selection process from precinct caucuses to primaries up to state conventions. Thus if any minority group did not believe a presidential candidate represented it, it could field its own slate and try to get that minimum 15 percent of the vote in a precinct or other electoral unit.

This also meant that in the 1976 primaries the new reformers would have to share delegates with conservatives in areas where they had once expected to get all the seats, though they would pick up delegates in areas like the South, where they once were shut out completely. However, a well-organized maverick movement, led by George Wallace or some other popular independent, might well be the major beneficiary.

In any case, the system of proportional representation seemed likely, in most instances, to splinter delegates among many candidates and probably lead to a stalemate at the convention, with no contender polling a majority. As a consequence, a settlement might very well occur in the back rooms after a few ballots, excluding the reformers and souring the electorate. Ironically, the new reforms thus threatened to take the nomination away from the voters and restore it to the bosses. These were risks, however, the reformers were willing to accept because the new system guaranteed their continued presence in the party.

The new rules proved that the party had opened up and there was no turning back. As a *New York Times* correspondent wrote: "The political consciousness of the Democratic forces had been raised in short-lived victory last year, the combativeness of traditional power had been raised in defeat. Together they needed a framework of accommodation, and, in the new rules, they seem to have found it."[6]

In fact, most party factions heartily approved the rules — except for COPE and the Coalition for a Democratic Majority, who feared that the old-line labor leaders and the regulars would lose authority. Still the system of proportional representation guaranteed a chance for everybody to gain some power. The edict to include minorities was, in a sense, non-ideological, though it might prove more difficult for conservative presidential contenders to put into effect than for liberals. Curiously, though, Wallace strategists figured that the proportional representational system would enable them to collect delegates all over the country in 1976. Under the new rules, too, the new caucuses — the National Women's Political Caucus, the Congressional Black Caucus, the caucus of progressive unions, the New Democratic Coalitions, the Puerto Rican, Chicano, Indian, and Gay groups — all drew a second breath, a chance to stay alive politically.

What was historically the most interesting of these events, however, was that the reform processes were no longer limited to the Democratic Party, but had spread into the protected highlands of the Republican Party. That was indeed a surprising development, for the progressive movement in the

Republican Party had fallen on bad days after Rockefeller's roughing-up at the Cow Palace in San Francisco in 1964, and after Nixon's election in 1968. Yet, in 1972, the reform caucuses, helped by sympathetic Republican progressives, managed to extend the principle of minority guidelines into the Republican Party rules, through two main forces, the Ripon Society, the iconoclastic organization of liberal Republicans, and the National Women's Political Caucus, whose small contingent of Republican women stirred up enormous public concern about the sexist practices of the party.

What really gave impetus to the changes, however, was the Committee on Delegates and Organization (called the "DO" Commission) set up in 1969 to consider ways of improving the convention's procedures and of implementing the party's Rule 32, which outlawed discrimination in party affairs because of race, religion, color, or national origin. The DO Commission made ten recommendations in 1972, seven of which the Republican Convention adopted. Many were similar to the McGovern-Fraser guidelines.

The two most important new rules the convention agreed to were Rule 32(a), which called for "positive action to achieve the broadest possible participation by women, young people, minority and heritage groups and senior citizens in the delegate selection process"; and Rule 32(c), which stipulated that "Each state shall endeavor to have equal representation of men and women in its delegations to the Republican National Convention." The convention then set up the so-called Rule 29 Commission, headed by Congressman William Steiger of Wisconsin, a moderate, to "review, study and work with the states and territories relating to the Rules adopted by the 1972 Republican National Convention," and to report back in 1975.

The Steiger Commission denied from the outset that it was another McGovern Commission. I spoke to Steiger about his committee in his congressional office one day in early 1974. Steiger, a delicately featured young man with sandy hair, spoke in a lucid and careful manner. He did not wish his commission to be viewed as a bunch of rowdies about to instigate a Chicago '68 or a Miami '72 in the Republican Party.

We are not like the McGovern Commission at all. First of all, we don't have an independent mandate to make recommendations that must be enforced immediately as the McGovern-Fraser Commission did. We must give our findings to the Republican National Committee, which is the final arbiter. Second, we don't have language suggesting or setting up quotas in our rules. The phrases singling out various minorities in Rule Thirty-two (a) was rhetoric to emphasize our interest and concern about these groups, not to artificially set them aside as blocs to be allocated seats on the delegations in a mandatory way. We don't wish to preclude any group of individuals from participating.

In any event, the state parties alone will decide in the end what "positive action" they will take in reference to these various groups and what that is is not clear yet. The Republican Party is leaving all those interpretive decisions to the states' own Rule Twenty-nine Commissions [those units set up to implement the reforms] which are being established now. Our party believes that the state parties are the unit of organization which must decide.[7]

Steiger's account of the commission's role and his interpretation of Rule 32(a) brought dissent from one of the reformers I talked with who originally helped spur the changes. Bobbie Greene Kilberg, a spunky young woman in her late twenties, who was the only Republican vice-chairwoman on the National Women's Political Caucus, adamantly rejected the notion that the language describing minority groups in Rule 32(a) was mere rhetoric. She insisted that the intention of the convention was to single out these constituencies that had been dramatically underrepresented at prior conventions, and, in using the words "positive action," to mandate that the party and the states set up affirmative-action programs to include these specific groups in the 1976 delegation.[8]

In other areas, Republican progressives were quietly nudging open the party's doors to minorities and reformers. The Ripon Society brought a lawsuit to declare unconstitutional the delegate selection formula adopted at the 1972 convention — a formula that favored small states in the South and West over the larger states of the North and East. The suit is not yet settled, but if Ripon wins, the decision would lead to a greater proportion of delegates from the large progressive Republican states, and, consequently, more minorities and reformers. The Republicans still have to take a few more steps — defining "positive action," establishing voluntary or affirmative action plans, persuading the rank and file that the Rule 29 Commission is not a McGovern commando mission to blow up the Republican Party. But the new caucuses finally have the keys to the party. It seems only a question of time before they use them to fling the party's doors wide open.

The press coverage of these historic transmutations has been, oddly, almost nonexistent. The pundits have behaved once again as they did after the original McGovern Commission set down its instructions: they hear nothing, see nothing, write nothing. For all the reams of copy devoted to Nixon's Silent Majority, Nixon's Southern Strategy, Nixon's Middle America, no one has picked up on the import of these new guidelines — that they are counterrevolutionary in the Nixon-

The Parties Reform

Ford Republican Party. The party has to integrate affirmatively into its ranks by 1976 the same dissident minorities it has made a spiritual crusade of denouncing for the past decade or longer. The party of the upright and decorous is veering dangerously toward its own possible internal blow-up — certainly not so raw and bloody as that which occurred in the Democratic Party, but still unsettling and jarring.

It is clear, then, that the progressive caucuses have now gained a foothold in both major parties. The question is whether these caucuses will have the stamina to keep plugging for increased representation in both parties in 1976. Will the Democratic reformers have the resources and commitment, for instance, to prepare for the entry requirements of the state delegate selection processes and to participate in them? Can the Republican reformers put pressure on their state parties to implement affirmative action programs? It is on the answers to these questions, it appears, that the fate of the movement hangs. They alone will indicate the actual impact of the reforms on the ideologies of both parties. As Dr. Donald Walters, the black Chairman of the Political Science Department at Howard University in Washington, D.C., concluded in a succinct analysis of the Democratic approach:

> The success of the new system will depend on whether all groups within the party increase their level of participation. Blacks and other minority groups must be vigilant as state parties establish their affirmative action and delegate selection plans and must develop their own positions on the contents of these plans. They must seek to find ways to place blacks and other minorities in strategic positions in state parties, and within the

national administrative structure of the Compliance Review Commission.

He added, "It is highly questionable" whether the new system will be "beneficial to blacks who want to participate in the Democratic Party."[9]

Other reformers were alert to similar perils. In early 1974, I talked with one of the Democratic Party reformers, Alan Baron, who edits the tart newsletter put out by the liberal Democratic Planning Group in Washington, D.C. A caustic critic of the party in the past, Baron was modestly reassured that the Democratic Party's new rules of 1974 represented the basic 1972 theme that women, blacks, and others should be adequately represented at its conventions. But Baron was a reformer without illusions. He emphasized, with a shrug of his shoulders:

> The reason why the regulars have acceded to the rules is because they are no longer frightened of bringing in women, blacks, the young, and other minorities. They realize that the reforms are neutral and that they can select their own loyalist caucus representatives and they can also manipulate the rules and pack the delegations. In short, the reforms are procedural, not substantive. They work for whoever is best organized and no longer guarantee success only for the progressives in the party.[10]

Bobbie Kilberg, the NWPC vice-chairwoman, concurred in the Walters-Baron view. She had acted as a consultant to the Republican Rule 29 Commission and plotted the various tactics that Republican reformers were using to hasten the new rules. Though by early 1974 she had made some headway in the battle for changes, she said that the new rules were no panacea for progressive woes: "They are mechanical corrections. They will make the party accessible to different groups, but they do not guarantee an automatic liberalization of the Republican Party."[11]

While much of the success of the reform delegations will depend more, perhaps, on whether they find attractive candidates for 1976 than on the strength of their own organizations, nonetheless the reforms in both parties do give minorities and progressives, at a minimum, some of the bricks and mortar to construct potentially strong edifices. The question really becomes: how hungry are the reformers for political power? Are they as determined as they were in 1972? And how famished are the conservatives?

2 ☆

The Women Rebel

ALL THROUGH the sixties there were portents of a women's political uprising. Betty Friedan's angry book about the psychic travail of being a female in America, *The Feminine Mystique*, struck an enormous response when it was published in 1963. By mid-decade, feminists had instituted a wide variety of court actions to obtain equal salaries and fair job opportunities. The National Organization for Women (NOW) emerged in 1966. By the decade's end, a crusade to enact the long-delayed Equal Rights Amendment had gathered energy. All these activities brought women closer to becoming a potent political force.

Early in 1971, *The New Democrat* was drawn abruptly into the issue of discrimination against women in politics. In March 1971, we published excerpts from a legal paper prepared by Phyllis Segal, a young student at Georgetown University Law School in Washington, D.C.[1] Ms. Segal's argument, heavily buttressed by figures, showed how the American political structure discriminated against women as delegates, candidates, and political appointees in both parties.

At the 1968 Democratic Convention, for instance, only 13

percent of the delegates were women; at the Republican Convention, only 17 percent. And only one of the 108 Democratic delegations was chaired by a woman: Representative Edith Green led the Oregon delegation. No Republican women at all represented New Hampshire, West Virginia, or the Virgin Islands. Two Democratic delegations approached a representative proportion of women: Florida with 44 percent, because of a state statute requiring equal division between men and women, and the Canal Zone with 50 percent. Neither party had ever had a female national party leader, treasurer or counsel.

Ms. Segal contended that the underrepresentation of women in parties "must depress the sense of political efficacy of all female citizens." The only activities open to women were dealing with other women or doing clerical work. Even the McGovern Commission (on which her husband served as chief legal counsel), she noted, though mandated to "assure broader citizen participation in the delegation selection process," had "3 women members out of a total of 28 (or 11 %, an even smaller portion than at the 1968 convention)."

Ms. Segal concluded that her statistic compilation only "touches the surface; an analysis of women in county and district party organizations and conventions would reveal a sinister pattern of underrepresentation in decision-making positions. On all levels of the political process, women play subordinate roles if they are represented at all. Consequently, women are not exerting proportional influence in determining who will run for office, and what policies the political parties will bring to government."

The study aroused the ire of *The New Democrat*. We ran an editorial, entitled "2nd-Class Democrats," in which we plucked from Ms. Segal's thesis the basic theme that "women today are second-class citizens in the decision-making bodies of the Democratic Party." Our editorial condemned the party's "discrimination" and its "abysmal neglect" of women, forecasting that the failure to bring about the immediate involvement of women in the party would lead to a "new Chicago in 1972."

Phyllis Segal's article had widespread reverberations. Within a few days of publication, our offices were swamped by requests for copies. In the same month, Gloria Steinem, at a meeting of the Democratic Policy Council, pointed to the paucity of women serving on the policy group and cited the Segal study as evidence of the party's pervasive bias against women. Segal's careful documentation led to a unanimous council resolution calling for "equal representation of women on all Committees and in all positions of influence in the party" and a promise from the embarrassed chairman, Senator Hubert Humphrey, to redress the imbalance of women on his own policy commission.[2] Over the next months, other female reformers began to draw from the Segal report to strengthen their arguments for 50–50 delegations and for a strict interpretation of the McGovern guidelines.

The most damning evidence of discrimination, however, was already on the public record: namely, that women were almost 53 percent of the nation's population, exceeding males by 5.5 million (mostly in the over-sixty category), but at the beginning of the seventies, there were only twelve female representatives, one female senator, and no female governors.[3] Women overall held less than 3 percent of all the elective offices in the United States.[4]

The rising public consciousness of this pattern of discrimination soon built up enormous pressure to form a women's political organization. In July 1971, as the time neared for the 1972 major party conventions, a group of female leaders, liberal Democrats, antiwar activists, feminists, and a few intrepid Republicans, met in Washington to create the National Women's Political Caucus (NWPC). They set up the organization as a bipartisan political arm of the women's movement, seeking the election of women Republicans and Democrats (as well as males who were sound on women's issues) to political office. Among the convenors were Representative Abzug, Gloria Steinem, Betty Friedan, Elly Peterson, former Republican National Vice-Chairwoman, and 300 or so other female leaders from twenty-nine states.

The New Democrat briefly noted the formation of the NWPC, but, perhaps reflecting liberal Democrats as a group, we were not at first aware of how great NWPC's impact might be. The national press, too, I might add, dutifully reported the fact of the NWPC's founding without comment. The handful of observers in the media who really understood what was going on were mainly women. They were aware that the women's movement had gone through much turbulence and internal feuding over the past decade, and that even the best liberal alliances crumbled apart after a year or so. But they were sure that, while no modern precedent for this kind of female political gathering existed, the NWPC was to be something different.

The July convention, in fact, defied all odds by bringing together an eclectic gathering of female groups — from the sedate to the moderate to the extreme, from the B'nai B'rith to the American Association of University Women to the Women's Strike for Peace.[5] All quickly agreed on common feminist goals: passage of the Equal Rights Amendment, the tripling of the number of women in Congress in 1972, the seating of women as at least 50 percent of all delegates at both conventions, and the changing of a whole grab bag of laws that affected a woman's sexual and economic life. The convention also broadened its agenda beyond strictly feminist issues by asking for an immediate stop to the Vietnam War and an end both to the use of physical violence as a way of resolving conflict and to the harassment of individuals advocating social change.[6]

The mood was fervent. Gloria Steinem said, "No one gives away political power. It must be taken. And we will take it."[7] Betty Friedan noted an analogy to the civil rights movement of the sixties. That movement "had to demand black power if the rights were to become real for most blacks. Women's participation in political power will change the politics of the nation in 1972 and thereafter more basically than the black movement or any minority ethnic bloc of the past."[8]

For all its enthusiasm, however, the NWPC's founding convention left a number of problems unresolved. There were differences between feminists and liberals over whether the NWPC should aim its efforts at correcting sexist injustices alone or whether it should support a broad progressive platform on the theory that all social issues are fundamentally feminist. The conflict went to the heart of the women's movement. On the one side stood Betty Friedan and her organization, NOW, which had attempted, quite successfully, to reach middle-class women on sex-discrimination issues, treating women, conservative and liberal, as a single group and remaining aloof from broader ideological politics. On the other side stood Bella Abzug, who argued that prejudice against women was inextricably bound up in the whole "white, middle-class, elitist, male" culture, and that one had to change everything about American society — its poverty, its racism, its imperialism — before one could change its sexism. This stance was the greater threat to the housewife's conventional values. In the first round, Abzug won, but the argument continued to complicate the caucus.

Republican women also had troubles with the NWPC's various planks, many of which were anti-Nixon. Bobbie Kilberg explained to me that "more Republican women perhaps would have joined the NWPC immediately if it had concentrated on the Equal Rights Amendment and other feminist problems and stayed away from the war." Kilberg was at first put off by the original NWPC members' list. "They were mostly New Democratic Coalition types. Bella Abzug and Betty Friedan had simply invited their friends in." But, she continued, Abzug convinced her that the organization had to be truly national, so she persuaded her Republican friends to join. "I recruited people and so did Elly Petersen. Petersen got prestigious women like Helen Bentley, head of the Federal Maritime Commission, to become members. However, some Republicans, like Anne Armstrong, Nixon's White House counselor, continued to regard NWPC as communistic because of its NDC orientation."[9]

What finally made the NWPC acceptable to Republican women was the decision of Jill Ruckelshaus to fill the role of spokeswoman for the Republican members of the NWPC. This occurred in February 1972, when she was a special assistant to Anne Armstrong in the White House and her husband, William Ruckelshaus, was director of the Environmental Protection Agency. Her standing in the party was respectable enough to encourage other women, like Anne Richardson, wife of the attorney-general, and Rita Hauser, former U.S. delegate to the United Nations, to work with the NWPC. Together with Helen Bentley, these three women began to travel around the country, carrying the message of women's issues, party reform, and delegation selection to gatherings of Republican women. Their speeches stoked the indignation of many Republican women against their state party leaders for failing to include more females in the delegations to the 1972 convention.

By the fall of 1971, the Republican and Democratic leaders began to plant organizational cuttings of NWPC around the country. The Manhattan WPC began with about 700 women, and it grew quickly to become the richest, most influential, and most dazzling of all the local chapters because of its proximity to money, media, and celebrities. By the end of the year, WPC caucuses had formed in eleven states and Washington. By mid-1972 the NWPC claimed about twenty-six state chapters and 13,000 members.

At our *New Democrat* office, dispatches on local WPC activities started to flow in from our state correspondents. We also received periodic visits from female reformers active in the NWPC. Fascinated now by this still invisible but ever-expanding female political network, we commissioned an article on the new movement by a young free-lance writer turned women's activist, Pamela Howard, a one-time New York *Post* reporter. The piece she wrote for us on the NWPC in October 1971 admirably captured the intensity and vibrancy of the women's crusade.

For the past six months, coincidental with the organization of the National Women's Political Caucus and a general consciousness-raising about the oncoming political year, women have been redirecting their energies. They are gearing themselves for a strong battle in the political arena, organizing at the grass-roots level, refusing to waste themselves for male candidates . . . Nonpartisan groups of women lawyers are organizing to make legal challenges to delegations that do not have a proportionate amount of women delegates. Plans are afoot to see that women are appointed to the credentials committees. Local and national fund-raising has begun.

The pulse beat was high, Ms. Howard wound up, because "women need a crash-course in politics. The handbook will be 1972."[10]

Pamela Howard's prognosis was essentially correct, but the first entries in the handbook actually came in the fall of 1971. The NWPC at that time set to work for the Equal Rights Amendment. The Washington office of NWPC mobilized the major women's groups, including NOW, the Federally Employed Women, and even the Women's Christian Temperance Union.[11] Then, a short while later, President Nixon announced that two Supreme Court justices were retiring. The White House said only that several "qualified men" were being considered. The NWPC at once demanded the appointment of two women, and produced a list of qualified female appointees. A controversy mushroomed over the insensitivity of the Nixon presidency toward women, and the NWPC splashed onto the front pages of the nation's newspapers.[12]

But what really transformed the NWPC into a mature political force was its decision that same fall to concentrate on delegate selection in both parties. That resolve, little publicized and lightly regarded at the time, proved to be a brilliant strategic move. It made it possible for both Republicans and Democrats to work together early on a common political project without partisan conflict.

The credit for the decision must rest with Congresswoman Bella Abzug. Abzug, for all the controversy she ignited, for all of her wide-brimmed hats, scatological comments, and sometimes strident manner, was an intelligent, seasoned political in-fighter, who knew how to dramatize issues, exploit opportunities, and transform women's politics into an emotional and widely publicized phenomenon. She, of all the originators of the caucus, imparted tactical direction and energy to the first uncertain steps of the NWPC.

One day in 1974, Ms. Abzug reminisced about the early days of the caucus. Sitting alone in her chaotic congressional office — somewhat like a dormitory room at college, with awards, stickers, books all strewn about — Bella Abzug appeared far more vulnerable and motherly a figure than the person whose fierce visage was often printed in magazines under the caption "Battling Bella." Ms. Abzug was remarkably temperate in private, small in stature, and almost tender of expression, a little perplexed at all the hostility her style elicited. Nonetheless, one could feel under her controlled emotions a sharp, intense fire, seeping out like the heat from a tightly shut furnace.

"In the fall of 1971, we didn't have the strength to run a woman seriously for the presidency. The only politics left to us was delegate selection. There was no more clearly defined or visible issue with which to energize the NWPC. It crossed party lines; it demonstrated the women's political role; it was a great organizing vehicle."[13]

Abzug rushed the idea through the NWPC Executive Board. By late fall of 1971, she had two separate NWPC delegations ready to press the case for 50–50 delegations with both party chairmen, Lawrence O'Brien for the Democrats and Senator Robert Dole for the Republicans.

The O'Brien meeting in mid-November 1971 turned out to be historic. Without an argument, O'Brien astonishingly abandoned all resistance to the delegation, headed by Abzug. He agreed to instruct state parties that half their delegations should be women and that any delegation not meeting the 50 percent standard "will be subject to challenge and must then prove that the process by which the delegates were chosen was open and nondiscriminatory." Abzug expressed bewilderment at O'Brien's quick capitulation.

> We knew no affirmative action programs for women could be set up and implemented so close to the time of the convention. So we simply demanded fifty percent women. O'Brien probably acquiesced so easily to our demands because, I think, he did not really believe our forces could organize women very rapidly and he did not really understand the propulsion of the women's movement. He underestimated us, as most people did. The battle was won there, before we even went to the convention. In retrospect, the fifty percent figure got us in trouble over quotas and we may have made a mistake. But in late seventy-one, we had no time to wait for affirmative action or compliance machinery to be set up.[14]

In December, a delegation of eight Republicans from the NWPC, including Bobbie Kilberg and Elly Petersen, prodded Republican chairman Robert Dole over the absence of women in the 1972 delegations. Dole disclaimed responsibility, saying the party had "no damned McGovern guidelines," but he agreed to try to persuade Republican leaders on the subject. He insisted, however, that the 50 percent compliance be "voluntary" because it was "right," not because it was part of affirmative action or of quotas.[15] This qualification crippled the party's commitment from the outset, for few states felt any compunction to make more than a perfunctory gesture on a purely "voluntary" matter. (Nonetheless, in 1972 women delegates rose from 17 percent to 30 percent at the Republican convention.)

The NWPC, in conjunction with the League of Women Voters, then set up and funded the bipartisan, tax-exempt Women's Education for Delegate Selection (WEDS). This unit sent women around the country in early 1972 and kindled the fires of the women's uprisings. It alerted women to delegate meetings, state conventions, and the 50 percent representation requirement; it also brought pressure on presidential candidates to "balance" their slates. *The New Democrat,* from its scattered stringers, began to put together the picture of a widespread and largely successful NWPC onslaught on the state Democratic parties. Indeed, most of the effort of WEDS, perhaps 80 percent, was directed at the Democratic selection procedures because of the guidelines. The Republican involvement was minimal.[16]

The presidential candidates soon intruded on the NWPC's harmonious delegate hunt. One of NWPC's own, the tenacious, willful, and articulate Representative Shirley Chisholm, declared her candidacy at the end of 1971. Ms. Chisholm granted an interview to *The New Democrat's* correspondent, Laurie Lazar, in November of that year. Her messianic campaign style had disturbed even members of the caucus, though the candidate herself always had the wit to recognize that her monomania might unnerve others. She told Ms. Lazar: "I always knew that when I would emerge nationally — because I always felt that someday I would, I don't know why, but I always did — I knew I would cause a stir . . . people either love me deeply or they detest me. You see, most people don't have the middle of the course with Shirley Chisholm." She planned her crusade to "bring us together . . . I am a part of the new politics in this country. I am a peace candidate. I am a woman's candidate. I am a black candidate. I mean, you name it and I am the one person that is in a very unique position today in America . . ."[17]

It was becoming evident that, because of Abzug's ecumenical philosophy toward both parties, the leaders of the NWPC wanted to stick strictly to delegate selection and stay far away from presidential politics. Thus, the NWPC was in a turmoil about Chisholm's jump into the presidential thicket. The pantherlike agility of Bella Abzug, however, finally brought order to the NWPC position. The caucus agreed to "strongly support" Chisholm but not to endorse her or anybody else, because the NWPC could be effective only as a pressure group if it could work within "all parties." (State and local chapters were still free to back whomever they chose.) Chisholm lashed out angrily at the caucus' neutrality and had bitter words for Abzug.

The NWPC did take a few more steps into the waters of presidential politics by meeting with all the candidates (except those who refused — George Wallace, Wilbur Mills, Henry Jackson, Richard Nixon, and John Ashbrook) and giving evaluations of them in *Ms.*, the slick new feminist magazine. Richard Nixon, it disclosed, was "neither a ladies' man nor a women's rights advocate . . . Nixon's attitude toward the NWPC was one of ridicule." Jackson, Vance Hartke, Wallace, Sam Yorty, and Ashbrook all received zeros; they showed "persuasive evidence of a lack of commitment to women's issues." McGovern and Chisholm rated highest.[18] In fact, Abzug, Gloria Steinem, and Betty Friedan were already debating among themselves whether to run as Mc-Govern or Chisholm delegates.

We were trying, at *The New Democrat*, to keep the activities of the women's movement under sharp scrutiny. We were aware that the women were plotting further forays into both conventions to challenge delegations, to fight for rules changes, and to raise the feminist flag, but we suffered from the infirmity that afflicted even major newspapers — lack of reliable access to the decision centers of women's politics. In trying to penetrate the operations of the NWPC, we often got mired in the bedlam of the NWPC itself.

We spent several months trying to persuade the Washington office of the NWPC to write a piece for *The New Democrat* on what its field hands were up to. The headquarters were in a perpetual state of frenzy. The staff changed almost daily. After hearing nothing for months, we concluded that the likelihood of any response was nil. Then we suddenly received an article for our April 1972 issue by one of the NWPC staffers, Deborah Leff, on "The Politics of Sex."

Ms. Leff gave a detailed list of items that NWPC partisans were pursuing in 1972: a challenge to all states not in full compliance with both the McGovern guidelines and with O'Brien's promise of delegations that were 50 percent female; a lengthy presentation to both conventions on the need for women in the cabinet, in administrative and judicial positions; an end to discriminatory laws against women; finally, a "big burst at the National Convention in Miami, over a thousand women with 'Women Power '72' ribbons tacked under their campaign buttons . . ."[19]

The NWPC grew uneasy just before the convention. Anxiety prevailed among the female leadership about any of their projects' making a measurable dent in conventional politics. Bothered by a bout of existential uncertainty, the NWPC began to force-pump its presence into every major political event where women might play a role or raise an issue. Its two superstars, Congresswoman Bella Abzug and Gloria Steinem, now editor of *Ms.*, appeared in June at the Democratic Platform Committee meeting in Washington. They introduced a fourteen-point feminist program prepared by the NWPC and quickly cajoled the delegates into accepting most of it as a separate and distinct women's plank.

In June, I was working at the platform hearings in Washington for McGovern — by then the dominant candidate in the party — having just taken a leave of absence from *The New Democrat*. From the vantage point of the McGovern strategists (led by Ted Van Dyk of the McGovern staff), the presence of Steinem and Abzug, actress Shirley MacLaine, and a number of other forceful female personalities, was both exhilarating and intimidating. By now, the NWPC was an important organization to placate — it had elected many delegates and it represented an influential segment of the left, and it was a symbol to an even larger, though amorphous, constituency of women across the country. It had a capacity to attract volunteers, organize field operations, and raise money. Its views and McGovern's views were essentially the same. And most of its leaders were old friends of McGovern.

The NWPC was a potent presence — and most of the platform committee members, generally McGovern delegates anyway, acceded to all the requests of the NWPC without much debate. Even the Muskie and Humphrey — and some of the

Wallace — delegates raised little protest. For the first time in the party's history, a platform committee adopted a special women's plank.

There was one issue, however, on which McGovern himself refused to budge — abortion. Abortion was one of those smoking grenades that most politicians — even militant liberals — refuse to touch in the midst of a battle because it might go off in their hands.

In late June, during this platform hearing, McGovern met with twenty NWPC leaders to discuss the question. Both sides attempted to work out a compromise between Mc-Govern's wish for only a general reference to the issue and the NWPC's desire for specific language. McGovern relied on his friend Gloria Steinem to prepare a modified resolution. Steinem's compromise phrasing was finally distributed to delegates as part of the already completed women's plank, but, at the last moment, another McGovern friend, Shirley MacLaine, upset by the language, took it upon herself to snip off the Steinem compromise, and the delegates ended up approving everything but an abortion clause.[20] Outraged, the NWPC leaders finally salvaged some reference to the issue by introducing and passing a minority plank. This was a very unfortunate misunderstanding and later led to resentment against the McGovern staff among the NWPC leaders.

My path next crossed with the NWPC at the Miami convention. *The New Democrat* staff and the NWPC leadership both happened to take rooms at the Betsy Ross Hotel, a rundown establishment that had a tacky beach front and air conditioners like iceboxes. This arrangement was by courtesy of a mutual benefactor, the lively, mercurial, strong-willed philanthropist of the left, Stewart Mott. Mott, who had inherited millions from his late father, one of the largest shareholders in General Motors, gave generous support to most of the liberal causes of 1972 — including the NWPC, *The New Democrat,* and a number of other reform groups. Mott's donation enabled our magazine to put out a few extra convention issues and allowed fifteen or so women to set up offices at the Betsy Ross and wage a brilliant tactical operation for the NWPC. Without Mott's seed money, some believe McGovern's candidacy itself might have withered and disappeared long before Miami.

Because we were harbored in the same digs, I often stopped in at the NWPC's offices. There was always an electric storm of activity. The NWPC was trying to service the entire 1100-women delegation that had come to Miami. Women were rushing in and out with press releases, notices of special caucuses, and flash announcements. A switchboard was ablaze with lights; the headquarters kept in touch with at least one woman in every Democratic delegation. All-night planning meetings, at which tricky questions on procedure and other complicated issues were worked out, took place regularly. Sessions with each of the presidential candidates were held on the first day of the convention.

On the floor, once again as a McGovern platform whip, I observed closely the NWPC convention maneuvers under the formidable direction of Bella Abzug. The women fought on three fronts simultaneously: the credentials challenges, the platform "abortion" fight, and the vice-presidential contest. For an organization now only one year old, the NWPC's performance had an impressive élan, an expert head-counting operation, and an effective public relations offensive.

Women raised about half the challenges to the credentials

of various state delegations. Most of these were negotiated and won before the Credentials Committee. The NWPC participated vigorously in the ouster of the Daley delegation, which did not have a sufficient number of women. They lost the challenge to the South Carolina delegation because of McGovern's preoccupation with winning a crucial vote on the contested California delegates — but their battle vividly reminded Democrats of the need for state parties to seek out women and minorities as delegates through disciplined affirmative-action efforts before 1976.[21] In all, the NWPC's challenges that succeeded added another fifty women delegates.[22]

The contest over the minority abortion plank electrified the convention. At the predebate staff meetings, an intense argument erupted over the way to defeat the issue without hurting the candidate's standing with the NWPC. McGovern finally asked those of his supporters who could not in conscience vote against the the abortion language to abstain. This assured the plank's defeat. McGovern's people, however, did a clumsy job of choosing the speakers for and against the proposal. Gloria Steinem, prowling the floor for votes during the convention discussion, burst out in tears and fury against Gary Hart, McGovern's campaign manager, for permitting a "right-to-lifer," one of the ideological opponents of abortion, to castigate the proabortionists for "murdering fetuses." The emotional scene made national television.

Many NWPC members were later somewhat pleased to learn, as Gloria Steinem wrote, that, "even the McGovern strategists admitted that the plank would have won, had they not ordered a crucial margin of delegates to vote no."[23] In fact, the superbly organized NWPC reached into every delegation and lost the resolution by a close margin of 1569 to 1103. As an example of the ardor of NWPC workers, Martha McKay, a North Carolina delegate, argued with and proselytized among her delegation, thirty-seven Wallace members and twenty-seven uncommitteds, throughout the day and night, and garnered an incredible forty-six favorable votes and only eleven noes.[24] Though bitter over the abortion loss, the women did get the most comprehensive women's rights plank ever included in a major party's platform. And the convention also passed a rules change that alternated the chair of future conventions between the sexes.

The NWPC still felt twice shunted aside by McGovern — first over South Carolina, then over abortion. The women finally let out all their frustrations in the vice-presidential fight. All over the floor, they began a revolt against Mc-Govern's choice of Thomas Eagleton; the women wanted Frances "Sissy" Farenthold, who had almost captured the gubernatorial nomination in Texas. Astonishingly, Farenthold's struggle brought her in second to Eagleton, outdrawing long-distance runners like Senator Mike Gravel of Alaska. "In one final, glorious push," Steinem recalled, "our jerry-built system of floor contacts actually worked. Most of the women had never heard of Sissy Farenthold before Miami, yet they trusted their floor leaders' information enough to vote for another woman."[25]

Few internal squabbles disrupted this smooth NWPC operation. The most visible were generated by the prickly and volatile Betty Friedan. At the convention, she constantly jockeyed for position with the NWPC leadership. But most women I talked to in the NWPC subscribed to the glowing assessment made by Brenda Feigen Fasteau, a young NWPC

41

leader, who wrote: "We had gained the attention of women and men who had gone into the convention never having heard of the Caucus, let alone its objectives. Most important, we had earned the respect of women who, although they had been distantly sympathetic, now felt themselves a part of the Women's Movement. We had become a recognized force in Democratic politics."[26]

A few women later dissented from the self-congratulatory tone of some of the NWPC's leaders. Both Germaine Greer, writing in *Harper's*, and Shana Alexander, writing in *Newsweek*, lambasted the members of the caucus for capitulating on abortion. Nora Ephron, in a piece in *Esquire*, said: ". . . in a sense the major function of the NWPC was to be ornamental — simply to be there, making its presence felt, putting forth the best possible face and pretending to a unity that did not exist."[27]

The NWPC had achieved enormous public recognition — but clearly it came at a price of some damage to the campaign of the candidate it championed, George McGovern. There was no denying the power, momentum, and brilliance of the women's movement in commanding attention on its significant issues. But, in the public's eyes, the women seemed to be remembered only for "disrupting" a respectable political gathering with the abortion and credentials challenges and the vice-presidency fling. For example, McGovern could not give his acceptance speech until three in the morning, after most of his Eastern and Midwestern listeners had gone to bed, because of the delay caused by the vice-presidential contest. In many instances, there was an insensitivity among McGovern's own pledged females (and other groups) in publicly rebuking him for not accepting, at whatever political cost, the entire feminist program or the total National Welfare Rights Organization plan or some other special-interest ultimatum.[28]

On the other hand, McGovern did have a Hamlet side. By being agonizingly ambiguous, he permitted a well-organized minority to probe for chinks in his own armor and press through when possible. Even McGovern's campaign director, Frank Mankiewicz, agrees that the real fault was McGovern's own; he simply was not tough enough with his fervent ideological admirers.[29] The NWPC, in short, for all its putative immaturity, succeeded on its own merits as an able political lobby and rightly gathered recognition where it was possible. Its raw voting power and political chutzpah were two attributes that few politicians in the future were likely to forget.

The NWPC turned its energies next to the Republican Convention. An eighteen-member group, led by Jill Ruckelshaus, brought to the convention most of the same items the NWPC had taken to the Democratic Convention — the fourteen-point program, a demand for equal representation of women on all delegations and party committees, the controversial plank on abortion, and a resolution for day-care legislation, which Nixon had vetoed earlier in his term. They also had a petition signed by some forty conservative and liberal Republican women for feminist changes in the party, gathered by the anti-Nixon NWPC.

Jill Ruckelshaus, and an unlikely convert, the outspoken representative from Massachusetts, Margaret Heckler, spearheaded the platform fight. They managed over a three-day period to defuse the hostility of many women on the committee and engender an enthusiasm for a women's plank. Anna Chennault, the indomitable "Dragon Lady" of the Republican right, still wrathful over Nixon's visit to China, suddenly extolled the women's goals and proposed a women's caucus among Republican delegates. By the end of the hearings, the platform committee altered the preamble and praised women as professionals working outside the home as well as inside it. The committee adopted the whole NWPC plank, including day care, but excluded abortion mainly because of the turmoil this issue had created at the Democratic Convention.[30]

The press carried few stories about the NWPC's activity in the Republican convention and none that suggested the magnitude of what the women were trying to do. The only notable flap was caused by Betty Friedan's arrival. Though a vociferous Democrat, Friedan defied the NWPC's pragmatic, though tacit agreement that members attend only their own party's meetings; she argued that women should go as women, not as party loyalists. This was a continuation of her old feud with Bella Abzug over a broad-based feminist versus a strictly political approach. Friedan attracted brief national media coverage by disrupting a panel on child care to protest the dropping of abortion as a platform issue, but then left a short time after, claiming that nobody would listen to her.[31]

Where the NWPC really altered the landscape in the Republican Party was in the arrangement for the future selection of delegates. Under pressure from Republican liberals in the NWPC, from the Ripon Society and liberal legislators, the convention agreed to amend the party's Rule 32(a). This rule had previously urged that "everyone" should participate in the Republican Party. Now it defined "everyone" broadly to include "women, young people, minority and heritage groups and senior citizens." To this, the convention added Rule 32(c), which further defined female participation by stating that "each state shall endeavor to have equal representation of men and women in its delegation to the Republican National Convention." Finally, the convention encouraged "positive action" by the states "to achieve the broadest possible participation." The meaning of all these rubbery phrases still had to be deciphered by the party's new reform commission, also established by the convention, the Rule 29 Committee. A tug of war was already beginning between the conservatives and the liberals over whether the 1972 changes were "rhetorical" or "substantive"; and the NWPC was organizing its own lobby to press for affirmative action in all fifty states.

Still, these were significant procedural changes in the party's rules, and it was somewhat surprising — though in keeping with an emerging pattern — that the national press paid so little attention to the liberalizing impact of the reforms inside the Republican establishment. It was particularly striking that a year-old caucus like the NWPC could influence the Republican Party at a time when Abe Lincoln's political legacy was replacing the Democratic Party in the South as the lily-white redoubt for conservatives and when the party's national crusade was to embrace all the elements of a silent majority, who detested militant women, long-hairs, blacks, and other minorities. A deep-seated identity crisis in the party, perhaps even an explosion, seemed to be in the making.

Thus, in both parties the pressures of the liberal NWPC were uprooting old political traditions in as permanent a way as a nineteenth-century Jacksonian Revolution, extending the office-holding franchise to wider and wider circles. For women, 1972 signaled the beginning of a new era, characterized most importantly by the rules changes in both parties, Mcgovern's nomination, and by the appointments of NWPC members Jean Westwood and, later, Mary Louise Smith to head, respectively, the Democratic and Republican parties.

The NWPC, after the 1972 election, continued to fight in both parties for acceptance of its cause. In the Democratic Party, members testified at every hearing of the Commission on Delegate Selection headed by Barbara Mikulski, the tough and wily city councilwoman from Baltimore. They also decried the slowness of the Rule 29 Committee in the Republican Party to act on the question of women and they began to prod the states to set up their own local Rule 29 Committees. Ultimately, the Mikulski Commission, in early 1974, sanctified the official presence of women (as well as black, ethnic, and other minorities) by proposing affirmative action as an integral rite in the selection of delegates in all fifty states. The Democratic National Committee gave the final approval to the party's new marching orders by adopting the revised rules in mid-1974. Some Democrats in the NWPC were still upset that the old guidelines — which had guaranteed delegations of which women made up 50 percent — were removed. The Republican National Committee, which was now headed by a woman, had not settled the doctrinal issue of affirmative action by early 1975, though it was likely to adopt a voluntary system of compliance.

Despite the loss to reformers of the 1972 election, the NWPC soon accelerated its organizing crusade throughout the country. It held its first national convention in Houston, in February 1973, really the first political convocation by women in the century since Seneca Falls, New York, when women organized to get the vote. The period was a time of despair for liberals. Most were in disarray around the nation; many had sunk into depression over McGovern's disastrous defeat; Nixon had bombed North Vietnam during Christmas, compared the American people to children, vetoed and impounded indiscriminately, and issued edicts like a monarch, all without provoking much organized liberal opposition.

Yet, with little money, and at the risk of a public relations fiasco, the NWPC trudged ahead to Houston with brave insouciance. The Houston convention was ostensibly designed to shore up the NWPC's weak structure by ratifying a constitution and a new set of directors. In retrospect, however, it would seem that Houston actually played a more considerable role in again raising the consciousness of dispirited women around the nation. The meeting drew 1400 women from almost all the states; there were Republicans, Democrats, Chicanos, Indians, blacks, Catholic nuns, and labor unionists. It excited the attention of the nation's press and television. By its vivacious atmosphere and lively sessions, it once again reminded the public that militant women offered an active, progressive opposition to the imperial policies of Richard Nixon.

The Houston Conference did, however, have to wrestle for a time with its oldest dilemma: how liberal should it become? Should it take on a broad range of progressive programs or stick to feminist issues? Or should liberal issues be defined as feminist issues? It was a familiar debate, but in the enlarged NWPC it now involved small states and large states, the minorities, the middle class, Republicans and Democrats, the national office and the local chapters, cities and rural areas.

The NWPC eventually subscribed to a sweeping progressive manifesto (as in 1971) for new social programs, coming out hard against Nixon's impoundment policies. This resulted because the make-up of the delegates, from both parties, was overwhelmingly liberal. But some strict feminists remained unreconciled. They were, in the main, women from NOW, a number of conservative Republicans, and some representatives from the smaller states, all fearful of alienating the middle-class housewife.[32]

After Houston, the NWPC decided to throw its resources into the election of women from both parties in the 1974 congressional and statewide races and, in particular, for the midterm Democratic convention at the end of 1974. The campaign was entitled "Win with Women '74." The idea was another tribute to the sagacity of Bella Abzug, who was seeking, once again, a frame within which both the Republican and the Democratic factions of the NWPC could operate without ideological conflict.[33]

The NWPC, despite a chronic lack of cash, brashly gathered up its doctrinal resources, made alliances with other female groups, built up its supply of electoral gunpowder, kept its force on a state of alert, and began to plot how to speed the election of women to state and federal posts in 1974. One vehicle for organizing women was the Equal Rights Amendment, which, having passed the House in 1971 and the Senate in 1972, was now making the slow passage from state legislature to state legislature.[34] Other springboards for launching female political careers were the local NOW organizations and the state NWPCs.[35] Both boosted the flagging spirits of many women by being convenient political organizing vehicles. Sissy Farenthold, head of the NWPC in the mid-seventies, had lost the close primary fight for governor of Texas in 1972. She recalled, "When the caucus endorsed me in the governor's race it was a tremendous psychological lift . . . It does make things easier for a candidate to have a caucus behind her . . ."[36]

Sometimes local NWPCs intervened directly in state contests. In 1974, in Sacramento, the California chapter of the NWPC paid filing fees of $211 each for fifteen women running for the state legislature. Mari Goldman, chief consultant to the California State Joint Committee on Legal Equality, said that ten days before the filing deadline ". . . no women had filed and we were getting desperate. We put out the offer to pay the filing fees and it was incredible. I think something like 40 women contacted us. Somehow, it was the catalyst that made them decide."[37]

The curve upward for the election of women, however, was still a wobbly one. The highest number of women elected to the United States Congress was in 1961–62, when nineteen entered the House. The figure dropped to ten, eleven, ten, and nine in the succeeding elections. But in 1972, sixteen won seats, and in 1974, the number rose to eighteen. This up-and-down situation was reflected in state legislatures. In 1960, 346 women served in state assemblies; in 1970, 306.[38] A dramatic shift occurred in 1972–73, when the figures rose from 344 women to 441, a 28 percent upswing.[39] Many politicians I talked to expected that in the latter part of the seventies the Watergate scandal would hurt male candidates and help female candidates, because voters would look on women as the only politicians who could not be bought.

I paid a visit to the national offices of the NWPC in Washington in early 1974, almost a year after Houston, to find out how the "Win with Women" campaign was progressing. Though the offices were wedged into a few tiny rooms on the side of an old apartment building, the racket, noise, and enthusiasm were very high. Jane McMichael, the executive director of the caucus, had just hired a new political action director. The NWPC, Ms. McMichael explained to me, was funneling its resources (especially contributions from its 50,000 active members) into local contests, because issues like abortion and the Equal Rights Amendment were once again inflaming public sentiment, and the NWPC could protect its "franchise" only through majorities in the state legislatures.[40]

One of the chief obstacles to women who were seeking election, according to Ms. McMichael, was the chronic lack of money. Women were not in contact with big contributors, because of the small female labor force; and, if they did work, most of them held menial jobs. As a rule, too, women were not big givers because they lacked a tradition of political involvement. The most serious problem for women, though, was the continuing societal taboo against the aggressive female, a taboo that was just as deeply ingrained among women as among men. "If a man is aggressive and hard-headed," said Ms. McMichael, "it helps him. The woman who is these things finds they're held against her. At the same time, if she is womanly and quiet, she's considered not strong enough. The woman in politics has to tread this thin line."[41] Nonetheless, three times as many women ran for state legislative offices in 1974 as in 1972. And the 1974 elections seemed to affirm the NWPC's optimism; the total of women state legislators rose from 441 in 1973 to 587 in 1974, though the figure still represented less than 10 percent of all state legislative seats.[42]

Ms. McMichael left me with a mental image of mobilized masses of women, moving steadily into the local avenues of politics. But it is probable that the NWPC's influence will not really be felt until the latter part of the seventies or early eighties. Once solidly upper-class and well educated, the

The Women Rebel

NWPC is now linking itself to the Coalition of Labor Union Women in attempting to bring working-class women into its ranks. As the caucus grows more experienced, it will reach out to diverse groups of women and make frequent alliances with male and centrist organizations.

The NWPC has its own tangle of troubles to contend with in the decades to come — the Friedan-Abzug ideological split, the Republican-Democrat tensions. The NWPC still appears rigid and unbending in its political positions at times, and its spokeswomen often come across as shrill and hostile. Its relationship to the Middle-American housewife has been contradictory though it is, nonetheless, an expanding kinship. Women in the NWPC have also, on occasion, proven just as capable as males of arranging selfish political deals that have hurt the women's movement and the progressive cause overall. Finally, like any caucus, the NWPC sometimes tries to do too much too soon without first solidifying its base.

Still, as evidenced by its steady growth in members, the NWPC is satisfying some felt need in the American body politic. It is becoming one of the true liberalizing forces in both parties. It is emerging as a platform for women to run on at all levels of government. It has the energy to assist in the presidential drives of progressive candidates. It may soon start to affect the fundamental voting patterns of female voters. Politicians no longer dare trifle with the National Women's Political Caucus.

3 ☆

The Blacks Organize

Together we stick,
Divided we're stuck.

Slogan adopted by the
Coalition of Southern Black Mayors

THE BLACK political movement, the successor to the old civil
rights movement, was still in its infancy in the early 1970s.
Black representation among Democrats in Congress was gradually increasing: six in 1966, eight in 1968, thirteen in 1970,
sixteen in 1972, seventeen in 1974 (these figures include the
one non-voting representative from the District of Columbia).
There was one black in the United States Senate, the only
Republican black in Congress, Senator Edward Brooke of
Massachusetts. At the state and local level, the number of
black elected officials jumped 152 percent from 1969 to 1974,
from 1185 to 2991.[1]

But with the disappearance of the magnetic and influential
civil rights leadership of the sixties, the new black political
ferment had no particular focus or outlet. Some outspoken
black mayors of large Northern cities had tried, without much
success, to assume the leadership mantle. Many organizers

were at work in the South, but they exercised only local influence. The blacks who really counted on the national scene were the dozen or so members of the House of Representatives,[2] and they took over the black leadership through the Congressional Black Caucus (CBC).

The CBC really grew out of the elections of 1968 and 1970. A number of new black legislators arrived just as the civil rights movement of the sixties was collapsing. They had the dynamism of the civil rights crusade in their blood; they came from heavily black districts, which gave them a powerful sense of identification; they felt a common alienation and anger in the white-dominated House.

In 1969 and 1970, they began informally to undertake some special assignments together: testifying against the Supreme Court nominations of Judges Clement Haynsworth and G. Harrold Carswell; meeting with Secretary of Defense Melvin Laird to protest discrimination in the armed services; lobbying with Speaker Carl Albert for better assignments for blacks.[3] They also unofficially anointed one of the senior blacks in the House, Charles Diggs, Jr., of Michigan, their chairman. But many of the early CBC projects flopped at the time, and few people ever read about or heard of the caucus.

The blacks in the House finally appeared on the national stage in 1971. In January, the Washington office for the Mississippi Loyalist Democratic Party telephoned *The New Democrat* to say that Aaron Henry, state chairman of the party, and Charles Evers, brother of the assassinated black activist, Medgar Evers, and now mayor of Fayette, were coming to the capital to lead a public lobby against the seating of five Mississippi congressmen.

The reason for the challenge dated back to 1968, when the

Democratic Convention had recognized the Loyalist Party, composed of blacks and white liberals, as the legal Democratic Party of Mississippi, and had ousted all the segregationist Democrats. In 1970, however, the five white Democratic representatives from Mississippi had refused to file with the Loyalist Democrats in their re-election campaigns, as required by state law. Aaron Henry and the local party leaders regarded this refusal as a public act of disloyalty to the national party and therefore grounds for the exclusion of the five from the House Democratic Caucus.

The Mississippi question quickly loomed, in our minds, as one of those rare issues that has the ideological wattage to illuminate an entire political landscape. The issue was one of such clear legality and such evident racism that it was difficult to understand how Democrats could duck it without condoning segregation or painting themselves into the darkest moral corners.

We obtained a copy of the legal memorandum on which Aaron was basing his challenge and printed it in our January issue in time to be distributed before the caucus vote. The memorandum spelled out the arguments against the Mississippi five:

When the five Mississippi Congressmen come to the House Democratic Caucus in 1971, they will not come as members of the Democratic Party of Mississippi recognized by national party, but as members of a party that has been rejected by the national party. Whether one calls them Dixiecrats, Wallace-ites, Republicans or what-have-you, the one thing that is clear is that *they are not Democrats* and thus have no place in a caucus of members of the Democratic Party and have no right to seniority assignments from that caucus . . . The issue before the House Democratic Caucus is simple. It can stand with the Henry-

Evers Democratic Party recognized by the national party and loyal to the principles of that party or it can stand with Governor John Bell Williams [former Democratic congressman ousted from the Democratic caucus in House in 1965 for supporting Goldwater] and seniority for segregationist Congressmen who are determined, as always, to wreck the national party's programs. On this issue, there can be only one decision — politically, ideologically, morally.[4]

Ostensibly, the occasion for the challenge should have been a dramatic one. One of the most vigorous black leaders in the House, Congressman John Conyers of Michigan, was in charge. White progressives in the Democratic Study Group were ready to back it up. I flew down to Washington, in a state of great anticipation, to take part in the intense lobbying efforts organized by the Mississippi Loyalists. But, suddenly, within days, the whole enterprise washed away in the swift undercurrents of political jealousies, lack of liberal organization, and black disunity.[5]

The principal problem was, ironically, the casual reliance by the Loyalists on the promises of one man, Congressman Conyers. Conyers simply couldn't put the pieces together. His resolution on the Mississippi five, first of all, did not fully satisfy the white progressives. Some of the New Yorkers, for instance, felt, quite incorrectly, that if they approved the new rules desired by the Loyalists, they themselves might lose seniority if they won office on the Liberal Party ticket. Conyers also confused his own political ambitions with the challenge. A driven, flamboyant, and vain man, he couldn't resist the press flattery that accompanied his crusade. Suddenly, he began running for Speaker against Carl Albert, and the whole Mississippi project got sidetracked. Other black congressmen, irritated with Conyers, dropped out of the enterprise. Finally, the white liberals, working through the Democratic Study Group, tried to patch together a last-minute compromise, approved by Aaron Henry, which would have established a caucus committee to investigate and fashion prospective rules for 1972. They intended to present the idea on the second day of the caucus. Conyers, however, dashed those hopes when he offered his resolution at the end of the first day of the caucus, after most of the liberals had gone home. He lost by 111 to 55.

The whole debacle was very disheartening, and many of the people involved in the struggle were frustrated. *The New Democrat* decided to run a story describing how the liberals had messed up the fight. We persuaded one of the women who had fought in the battle to write it. She preferred to appear under a pseudonym for fear that she might lose her job if some of the legislators who had been involved found out about her views. Her story, strongly critical of Conyers, prompted the congressman to call me a few days after the story appeared to berate me in heated language. I told Conyers that I had complete confidence in our reporter's work. Conyers was not mollified. Following that bitter confrontation, we did not speak for a long time.

The experience was painfully instructive. We came to expect angry rebuttals from offended United States congressmen as we tried to persuade the Democratic left to engage in common-sense politics; and it was, in a kind of backhanded way, flattering to our modest influence that elected officials wanted to engage us in debate over strategy.

Of course, there was always the possibility that Conyers was right and we were wrong. After all, we knew that the proposal would not pass under the brightest of circumstances. (In defeat, the resolution actually did gain fifty-five votes, or one-third of the party caucus, which was extraordinary, considering the ragged conditions of the balloting.) Conyers might have been correct to sense that the importance of the idea lay more in its being proposed than in the number of votes it got. So its last-minute, slapdash presentation was not critical if the impact was to be long-term, and unquestionably the resolution did stir party members to reassess their political values. It spurred some Democrats to think seriously about whether they should support segregationist congressmen who "passed" as party members; it forced some progressives to consider redefining the criteria of party affiliation.

And Conyers had some history on his side, too. A lonely, defiant black protest in the Democratic Party in 1964 had provoked a profound rethinking about party procedures. This occurred when the Mississippi Freedom Democratic Party (the same Loyalists of 1968) challenged the right of white regulars to be seated at the convention. This "uppity" action represented the first major attack against the racially exclusive Southern Democratic Party since Hubert Humphrey led the fight for a civil rights platform at the 1948 Democratic Convention. Howard Romaine, a young journalist in Atlanta, observed that:

Although many at that time judged the 1964 effort a failure, it set the stage for the seating in 1968 of a black and white integrated delegation, led by Charles Evers and Fannie Lou Hamer. But, by that year, the Southern black strategy of challenging racist and restrictive Democratic Party processes had become a national strategy for reform, as the McCarthy-led peace chal-

57

lengers tried to dump the Democratic establishment and its leader, Lyndon Johnson.[6]

That blacks should have initiated these cathartic outbursts was hardly surprising. Because of their small numbers and because of the resolute indifference of the country toward their plight, blacks were forced to practice a kind of *j'accuse* politics to draw public attention to their grievances. Their role inadvertently became the catalyst for basic internal reform in the Democratic Party, first at the national convention, and then in the party in Congress.

Whatever small satisfaction one might take from the Conyers defeat, however, one had to acknowledge that it showed the continuing weakness among black leaders — the failure to coalesce around a single objective and effectively thrust it into the public's vision. *The New Democrat's* approach, to emblazon the protest of the thirteen blacks and the dozens of white sympathizers across the front pages and fill the evening newscasts with outraged reports on Democratic Party racism, might have prevented the issue from slipping back into oblivion.

The congressional blacks were well aware of their lack of planning and foresight. Shortly after this incident, they displayed a fresh and innovative tactical sense. They shrewdly played on the weaknesses of the Republican politician in the White House, Richard Nixon. The CBC by now conceived of itself as the replacement for the defunct civil rights brigades of the sixties, and, in this sense, as an independent, nonpartisan body representing not the Democrats, but all of the country's blacks. Consequently, it accelerated the issuance of a series of requests to Nixon, begun quietly in 1970, for a meeting to discuss the conditions of black citizens in the

United States. Nixon turned down the CBC once again — as he had done in the past — because he regarded the caucus as a Trojan horse designed to catch him off-guard inside the walls of his citadel. Now, exasperated, the CBC decided to insult Nixon publicly, and all of the members agreed to boycott Nixon's State of the Union message in January 1971.

The press understood the symbolism of the gesture and gave spectacular coverage to the CBC's absence. A boycott by a small enclave of blacks in the House suddenly mushroomed into a major crisis, and discomfited Richard Nixon. Immediately, Nixon hastened to retrieve the idea of a meeting in an effort to appease the black community. Nixon may have believed the 1972 election in jeopardy, as one ethnic group after another became restive with him; but the boycott also occurred at a time when Nixon was especially vulnerable, just as the Gallup polls showed him falling behind Muskie in the presidential race. Nixon quickly dispatched a message through Senator Brooke for a conference. According to one presidential aide, he was now "quite prepared to recognize that the congressional blacks are the pre-eminent black leaders of the nation."[7]

The meeting on March 25, 1971, was a sham. The CBC presented Nixon with a memorandum of sixty-one demands, focusing primarily on the alleviation of the 10 percent black joblessness rate in the nation, and recommending the immediate creation of 1.1 million productive jobs in the public sector and a $6500 minimum income for a family of four. Nixon said nothing about the caucus' demands. He seemed intent on playing to the press by promising extra funds for summer work for teen-agers and some additional assistance to Negro colleges. The CBC members were dissatisfied with Nixon's gestures.[8]

A month later, Nixon made a formal reply to the CBC's

sixty-one demands. He cited revenue sharing and government organization as his notable contributions to the well-being of American blacks. One black congressman succinctly summed up his own feelings and those of his colleagues when he called Nixon's answers a "charade, a farce, a misconception, all kinds of trickery."[9]

The Nixon meeting, however, proved to the CBC leaders that, for the first time, they could use their small numbers to proclaim their grievances and publicize the abysmal economic situation of American blacks. This episode gave them a better appreciation of the fundamental moral sympathy they could draw on in the nation and the enormous symbolic value they possessed as the sole representatives of the nation's largest minority. In turn, the extensive publicity accorded to the caucus' joust with Nixon etched in the nation's voters a heightened awareness of a new progressive political group that had emerged among the nation's blacks, and which, despite ties to liberal Democrats, was now being assiduously courted by both parties.

But the blacks had not yet had time to formalize the caucus. In mid-1971, the tremendous national exposure of the White House meeting generated an overwhelming flood of demands for services and assistance from black communities around the country. The black representatives finally set up the CBC as an official structure, hiring a staff and research personnel to serve the nation's blacks and to oppose the administration more systematically in the future. A $100-a-plate dinner in Washington netted the CBC $250,000. Exultant over the success of the fund-raiser, the members established head-quarters in the Congressional Office Building and hired Howard Robinson, a former Foreign Service Officer and labor organizer, to direct it.

From our *New Democrat* office in New York, we could see only dimly the evolution of the CBC. Reams of publicity began to flow out of Washington, glowing with reports of the new successes of the CBC, but details about what the new caucus was doing day to day were hard to come by. One of the reasons for the lack of illumination, it later emerged, was that, from the outset, the CBC was hounded by deep and recurring troubles.

First, there was a foul-up over the dinner funds, and the initial paychecks for the CBC staff did not clear the banks; the offices were too small and cramped and the staff did not find adequate space for over a year; the requests from blacks continued to pour in relentlessly and couldn't be handled; Robinson himself perceived his role as primarily that of chief of protocol, so he met with myriads of local officials and set up outside hearings but neglected his CBC bosses, which irritated their congressional staffs.[10]

By agreement among its members, the CBC also settled into being a black version of the League of Nations, with much ceremony, little power. Each legislator could do whatever he or she wished within the CBC. The caucus arrived at an "official" position through an affirmative vote of two-thirds of its members, but such votes were not binding on the dissenters, and at times some members took a public stance in opposition to the caucus. Often, members claimed credit for legislation that the CBC itself had sponsored.[11]

In retrospect, it is clear that the early clutter and confusion at the CBC were inevitable. The new organization had a lot of headstrong personalities, a gelatinous structure, and a need to be something grander than a "PR" outfit — perhaps a kind of black presidium. Still, as far as the public image went, it *was* a winner. The CBC was persistently in the national eye.

Cover stories appeared in *Newsweek* and many black journals. Blacks began to use the caucus as a place to voice their frustrations and a means for receiving national coverage. The CBC held regular, well-publicized hearings around the country.

Our own thoughts at the time, unclouded by knowledge of the internal disorders, were that the simple existence of the black caucus was in itself a daily reminder to the Nixon administration and to Congress that a restless minority, numbering almost twenty million beings, was growing angry. Thirteen votes in Congress clearly were just so many drops in the ocean, but the CBC was beginning to act as a moral conscience for the nation — something which, in the amoral wasteland of the Nixon administration, was a considerable achievement. But what real impact — beyond the symbolic one — the CBC was actually having on the policies of the two major parties was another matter. In the Republican Party, after the hostile nature of the Nixon talks, the CBC became a pariah. In the Democratic Party, its mother party, the CBC also elicited a surprising lack of interest.

For example, in late 1971, the Democratic National Committee showed scant concern in placating the CBC or other black leaders over job hiring. Channing Phillips, the black National Committeeman from the District of Columbia, wrote a piece in *The New Democrat* on "Black Caucusing" in the Democratic National Committee, in which he condemned the "all deliberate speed" the committee's chairman, Lawrence O'Brien, was evidencing toward CBC demands for 20 percent of the positions on the staff of the party. Despite a visit by Coretta King, Mayor Richard Hatcher, and a number of CBC members, Phillips wrote, O'Brien failed to respond in any substantive way to the hiring or policy requests of the group. Phillips' angry assessment was "that Blacks must see the Larry O'Briens for what they are, and only a united voice and probably a demonstration of power in a more focused way (perhaps by mobilizing Blacks to sit out an election or to go third party) will command the respect and therefore response of the Larry O'Briens."[12]

An even more damning black indictment of the Democratic Party appeared in a symposium sponsored by *The New Democrat* in mid-1971. We sent out letters to a number of prominent black leaders and intellectuals in the country, including four members of the CBC, asking them to reply to the queries: "The Democratic Party has posed historically as the party of the minorities. Do you believe the party today is fulfilling this critical role? Is it possible for the Democratic Party to represent the black individual in the political process?"[13] The comments of the CBC representatives were raw, angry, exasperated, and hurt. The collective wrath of these replies shattered any feeling of self-congratulation that the Democratic Party might hold toward its championing of the minorities.

Congresswoman Shirley Chisholm wrote:

The traditional Democratic Party, like the traditional labor movement, is imbued with too much 1930's rhetoric and has become the symbol of the status quo. It makes no sense to talk about the New Deal to minority groups — as they know they got "no deal." Minority groups desire job training, education, and decent housing — that have largely been denied them. As the population shifts out to the suburbs there is less and less concern for urban issues — and let's face it, the cities, now ringed by white suburbs, are the center of American minority living. . . . The time has come when Blacks and other minority groups will respond only to leaders and parties, be they Republican or Democratic, who feel they have their interests at heart.[14]

Congressman Parran J. Mitchell of Maryland bitterly complained:

The Democratic Party has not done right by Blacks. We do not have our fair share of the party decision-making powers. We do not possess a fair share of the jobs in the Party organization. We do not receive our fair share of political appointments after we have contributed heavily to Democratic victories. Black candidates are not encouraged, do not receive substantive party funds when they run, and once elected are ignored . . . I think the lesson learned here is obvious. We are *always* Blacks first and Democrats second. The Republican Party isn't any better, but it doesn't claim to be. The Democratic Party regularly produces egalitarian rhetoric, and in practice behaves like the Republican Party.[15]

Congressman Ronald Dellums of California acidly summarized:

The Party has been historically portrayed as representative of the minorities, yet it has never dealt substantially with the critical problems which affect those constituencies or even seriously attempted to link up the problems of its several constituencies . . . These problems still exist. They exist in a large part due to expedient liberals in the Democratic Party — liberal expedient politics being that sort of politics designed to deal with the symptoms of problems while creating the appearance of dealing with the causes of those problems.[16]

Because of our own chronic idealism, and our abiding belief in the healing power of Democratic liberalism, the symposium was a jolt for *The New Democrat* staff. We summed up our bewilderment and surprise in an editorial commentary:

The extraordinary revelation about these replies is that, for blacks, the Democratic Party as constituted today has become a frustrating and, in some ways, regressive political institution (although the Republican Party is far, far worse). The complaints range from a feeling of persistent exclusion from the decision-making circles to a belief that the party's civil rights rhetoric is a token gesture to blacks, not a real acknowledgment of the core-racism of American society. Blacks have been forced to embrace the traditional, old philosophy, best stated by Missouri's black congressman, William Clay: "black people have no permanent friends, no permanent enemies, just permanent *interests* — in the future black people are going to look out for *their interests.*" This means that blacks will stay with the Democratic Party as long as it acts as a catalyst for their hopes, but they will leave the Party if it does not reawaken to the human anguish of Negro America . . . As the black leaders so plainly state in this explosive Symposium, they are no longer bound by myths, only by results.[17]

The blacks were fully prepared to follow their own dictum. They demonstrated this in their approach to the Democratic presidential politics of 1972. In the months that followed the symposium, *The New Democrat* discerned and published articles on the three tactical approaches that suddenly became fashionable among the CBC politicians as ways to gain influence in the presidential selection process: the Chisholm scenario; the Julian Bond "favorite son" plan and its Gary convention variation; and the "best white liberal" approach.

The Chisholm notion was to rally all the disenfranchised in the country — minorities, women, the poor — around her own candidacy and then take advantage of the Democratic Party reforms to pick off delegates in primaries around the country and enter the Democratic Convention with an immense hoard of votes with which to bargain for concessions from other candidates. In her interview with *The New Democrat* in the fall of 1971, Chisholm remarked: "My candidacy really means — all you helpless and powerless American citizens, you don't have to be helpless and powerless . . ."[18]

The strategy fell apart, however, when neither the Congressional Black Caucus nor the National Women's Political Caucus would agree to endorse Chisholm. Both caucuses were gingerly feeling their way into national politics for the first time. They were not ready to rush into supporting anybody's race for the presidency, especially a candidate whom many regarded as egocentric and unrealistic. Without their backing, Chisholm's effort faltered.

The second plan, set out by Julian Bond, was somewhat more palatable to many blacks. Bond wrote down his thoughts in a memo, which he circulated among his colleagues and which we published in *The New Democrat* along with the Chisholm interview. He argued that a black "favorite son or daughter" should run in selected states where the black vote was a factor. The goal was to "free Black politicians from dependence on any of the Presidential candidates; to invigorate Black voters through a campaign by a well-known, locally-based Black politician; to give Black delegates to the 1972 convention a bargaining power they had not possessed before."[19] The Bond proposal had certain attractive features: it gave visibility to home-grown black leaders and cost less money to undertake than a campaign for a single black presidential candidate. But it did not explain how local blacks would amicably agree on a particular "favorite son," nor did it really grapple with the harder political question of what to do when a sympathetic white liberal contender running in the primaries might be damaged by a minority opponent.

The Bond strategy collapsed of its own unreality. Like a

later AFL-CIO notion of running uncommitted slates in the Democratic primaries, the Bond idea ran aground on the basic political fact that people tend to go out and vote for a particular candidate, not for neutral delegates or favorite sons, because they do not like to waste their ballots. In any event, the blacks were not sufficiently well-organized to launch such an extensive enterprise of favorite sons or daughters.

A variation on the Bond suggestion emerged at the first National Black Political Convention in Gary, Indiana, on March 10 to 12, 1972, which attracted 4267 delegates representing black Nationalists, Christians, Muslims, reformers, Pan-Africanists, Democrats, and Republicans. The convention was an attempt to construct a national black coalition to exercise some leverage in the presidential election. It won the strong endorsement of Congressman Diggs, chairman of the CBC and the convention's co-convenor, along with Mayor Richard Hatcher of Gary, Indiana, and Imamu Baraka, the black nationalist from Newark, formerly LeRoi Jones, the prolific playwright.

The CBC initially was enthusiastic about the convention because, unlike the Bond idea, which involved a lot of money or resources to run dozens of black favorite sons, here, as Howard Robinson, the CBC Executive Director bragged, "we could really hurt the Democrats a lot by organizing 5 to 10 percent of blacks and urge them to vote Republican."[20] CBC members, however, gradually had second thoughts that the convention was going to slip out from under their control and might be seized by nationalists, separatists, or radicals. So the CBC voted not to participate as a body. Instead, five members attended by themselves; they were among the very few black elected officials present.[21]

Although the tone of the meeting was separatist, there was

67

no coordinated, dominant ideology. The Gary convention concluded with a manifesto that, while full of many good proposals, frightened the CBC leadership by calling for an end to busing and urging the United States to "dismantle" Israel. The CBC, concerned about its liberal standing — and therefore its ability to influence the progressives in both major parties — publicly repudiated both proposals after the convention and issued its own "Black Bill of Rights," containing an abridged version of its sixty-one demands made to President Nixon. In a further ploy to detract from the public attention Gary was receiving, the CBC stridently insisted that its agenda was "non-negotiable" by all presidential candidates.[22]

In reality, the only effective strategy remaining to the blacks as the Democratic Convention neared was the "best white liberal" candidate approach. This, in a sense, was inevitable. In a presidential primary campaign where only white candidates were contending seriously and where the dynamics of power politics demanded that, if you wanted influence, you had to endorse a candidate early, the blacks now had to turn to the leading white progressive candidate to carry forward their interests.

By this time, I had joined the McGovern campaign. In June, McGovern was closing in on a preconvention delegate victory. Much of the black leadership had already endorsed McGovern — Mrs. Coretta King, the Reverend Jesse Jackson,[23] and Julian Bond. Several talks at that time with black leaders convinced me that most blacks were ready to support McGovern and only a very few still clung to Humphrey.

Shortly after McGovern won the California primary, the CBC finally acted. Congressman Conyers candidly observed: "The [CBC] had to move fast before McGovern clinched the nomination without us. He had almost all the delegates he needed. And he told us he wanted the black uncommitted bloc of delegates to put him over the top by delivering the crucial 11th hour vote."[24] Thus, Delegate Walter Fauntroy and a few other CBC members appeared with McGovern at a June twenty-sixth press conference to announce the support of a national coalition of ninety-six uncommitted black delegates. McGovern said that he could now win in Miami. But the CBC's first venture into coalition politics was a bit disorganized; by the day's end — because of name duplications, angry delegates who said that Fauntroy had neglected to tell them what he was doing beforehand, and people who were already McGovernites — the list of black endorsers eroded to seventy-five, then, by the end of the week, to fifty-seven.[25]

Yet the CBC endorsement was in a way a landmark. McGovern, according to Congressman Clay, did agree, in exchange for the delegate support, to go along with the "spirit and substance of both the Caucus' Bill of Rights and the National Black Political Convention's Agenda."[26] However, McGovern had a propensity for vaguely promising acceptance without really spelling out what he was accepting. Clearly, his agreement in spirit did not mean endorsing the controversial pronouncements in the Gary document on busing and Israel, or the specific quotas for blacks on the Supreme Court, in the cabinet, or other posts. Delegate Fauntroy later publicly specified a commitment that seemed a more logical one for McGovern to make. It included a promise to undertake a $2 million black voter-registration drive and a pledge to give federal patronage to blacks in five key states and the nation's capital.[27] Later, McGovern publicly accepted the idea of an ethnic balance for blacks in the Democratic Party when, after the Miami convention, he named Basil Patterson, a black politician from New York, as one of the deputy party chairmen.

Whatever the exact contours of the CBC–McGovern pact, it impressed the Washington *Post*. The *Post* stated in an editorial, "Black Power Comes of Age," that the

> Black Congressional Caucus [has] become one of the most serious segments of black activist America . . . a number of politicians, notably Delegate Walter Fauntroy, decided it was time for blacks to move and to move decisively. Fauntroy and others began serious political negotiations with the McGovern people, not in the old framework of asking the candidates to say something good about brotherhood, but in the new mold of presenting black-developed demands and then bargaining for political *quid pro quo*. The McGovern camp wanted the votes and went along with much of the Black Congressional Caucus' Bill of Rights and other demands. Hard political bargaining ensued which seemed to satisfy everyone, whereupon Fauntroy, Congressman Louis Stokes and William Clay and others began rounding up some critical votes and then delivered them at a critical time.
>
> Not everyone was happy . . . But, politics, after all, is a matter of timing, and of adjusting strategies to meet shifting situations. In a sense, all of the critics may have been right and all of the things they call maneuvering may have been correct . . . no matter how McGovern fares, it did set in track a black mode of participation in the political process in this country which is not likely to be reversed in the near future.[28]

This new black mode of "participation," it seemed, rather strangely resembled the old white mode of politics.

The CBC exacted a considerable price from McGovern, but it was a skewered bargain because it did not actually affect his postconvention campaign. The CBC members (and all other black groups) were consigned to rather insignificant roles in the day-to-day direction of the McGovern presidential effort.

I knew a number of the black aides at work in the Mc-Govern operation. Perhaps the most important in the candidate's daily operations was Yancy Martin, the traveling aide to McGovern, an affable, dynamic man, who saw to it that ideas and speeches on black affairs were brought to the candidate's attention. Yet, on many occasions, the Washington office sent out to McGovern speeches on black issues that were slipped by Martin. (Of course, this happened habitually, too, to the candidate's white experts on the campaign plane.)

McGovern's non-traveling black advisors also had only tenuous contact with the candidate. Julian Bond, Jesse Jackson, Walter Fauntroy, and others met with McGovern from time to time — but their influence was superficial. The Mc-Govern people did not let themselves be crowded by their liberal interest groups — except publicly. Gary Hart, in his book on the campaign, unconsciously gave a revealing account of what McGovern's top advisors actually thought of their relationships with the black leaders — and practically all of the other liberal cadres of the period — when he described one incident that occurred during the Miami convention. He wrote:

> . . . I had been summoned to meet with black leaders who had become uneasy that they were not involved in something that even they could not define. Black leaders Walter Fauntroy, Willie Brown (a California State Legislator), Ken Gibson (Mayor of Newark), Jesse Jackson, and others, had consistently participated in campaign consultation and decision-making. But there still seemed to be growing restlessness and uneasiness throughout the campaign. It baffled me. Each special-interest group or caucus seemed to want to possess the campaign. There

seemed to be an unwillingness to accept the fact that the Mc-Govern campaign was an entity unto itself, that we solicited support (which was long withheld in crucial periods) from many quarters — blacks, Chicanos, women, youth — and made a supreme effort to seek involvement and participation in decision-making, but that we were not the creation or creature of any group.[29]

But the problem the blacks had, no matter how much they were attended to or soothed, was an understandable desire to nail the chronically confusing McGovern campaign to specific promises.

Thus, the CBC in the earlier stages of the campaign was more effective in fixing on paper the Democratic commitments than in placing blacks around the candidate. Still the black liens forced on McGovern by the CBC gave black people something to rally around and exert pressure with should McGovern gain office. In many ways, this was perhaps the most important event for the black community, more so even than the candidate's own deep personal commitment to civil rights and black advancement.

In the end, the central factor in the CBC's capacity to negotiate forcefully, though, lay in its ability to sell itself to both political parties as the foremost representative of black interests on a national level. It was the force of that position that eventually persuaded both President Nixon and Senator McGovern to seek out the CBC for prolonged discussions. Particularly in an election year, the CBC carried for all politicians the immense symbolic weight of representing twenty million people. And it was a constant reminder, especially to the Democrats, that 20 to 25 percent of their quadrennial presidential vote was black. The CBC happened politically at the right place, at the right time, with the right minority.

Ironically, a CBC endorsement influenced the presidential candidates more than the black voting patterns in 1972 — if anything, the endorsement perhaps had a negative impact. The proportion of registered black voters casting ballots for president dropped dramatically from 85 percent in 1968 to 58 percent in 1972 (when voter turnout overall was the lowest since 1948). Blacks split 87 percent for McGovern and 13 percent for Nixon, a sharp reversal from 1968, when Humphrey got 95 percent and Nixon 5 percent of the black vote.[30] A study of black party-identification carried out by the University of Michigan's Institute for Social Research shortly after the election reported that blacks choosing the Democratic Party slipped from 85 percent in 1968 to 69 percent in 1972, with 9 percent "leaning" Republican and 22 percent remaining independent. The study attributed this change to disillusionment over the results of the civil rights and antipoverty legislation, to the fact that more blacks were entering the middle class, and to feelings of political independence stimulated by the Gary convention.[31]

There was another and more frightening interpretation of the 1972 election: McGovern's calamitous defeat was, among some pollsters, attributable to the race issue. Daniel Yankelovich, who undertook election surveys for the *New York Times*, concluded from his figures just before election day that "there are twice as many Democratic defectors as usual and the defectors are twice as likely to resent some minority group gains." Or, as Jesse Jackson poetically put it, "The real issue is not the bus, it's us."[32]

The Yankelovich survey uncovered a problem of perhaps

shattering dimensions for the American reform movement in the decade of the seventies. The demon of race had already stormed into the election of 1968. In that year, Nixon narrowly defeated Humphrey, but George Wallace's racist campaign garnered 13.5 percent of the votes. In 1972, McGovern received only a slightly lower percentage of votes than did Humphrey in 1968 (about 4.6 percent less), but Nixon, once Wallace was out of the running, captured almost all the floating Wallace votes — and low-income white Democratic votes in addition — by the subtle racist pitches of his first administration.

The demon might, I believe, prove impossible to exorcise in the American electorate — or perhaps only a profound force like a depression might temporarily submerge it. In any event, the stark reality of the election returns in 1968 and 1972 dictated only one course for the CBC (as for any other black group): to pick up the philosophical cudgels dropped by the late Senator Robert Kennedy, who had preached the unity of the minorities and the blue-collar workers around common economic issues in order to overcome the corrosive impact of race on the country's elections.

The New Democrat had enunciated this sort of political approach in the magazine's first editorial, written by Grier Raggio. Raggio stated:

> Basically we feel that tough and effective liberalism, of the sort Robert Kennedy represented in his last months, is still the best foundation of government in this country. We are haunted by a photo of Robert Kennedy in Watts on the last day of the California campaign. He was standing on top of a car, surrounded by a bodyguard of the toughest ghetto blacks that ever made the pages of *Life*. Kennedy was building a coalition of traditional liberals and of the millions of people — Chicanos, poor whites,

blacks — shortchanged by the American system. We believe that coalition would have carried him to the Presidency and this country to better health.[33]

The CBC, in fact, soon after the 1972 election, began to shift toward a course of more pragmatic black-white coalitions. Partly, this was an awakening to the grim news of the 1972 contest. Partly, it was the fact that CBC members were getting older and therefore more practical in their ways and more eager to influence white voters as well as black ones for legislative purposes. Partly, too, it was the new opportunities caused by the Republican Watergate scandals.

In the fall of 1973, I attended the third annual CBC fund-raising dinner at Washington. The theme this time was explicitly coalition-building. The occasion glittered with the prosperity and self-confidence of the black political movements of the seventies. The ballroom, brimming with black celebrities in sports, entertainment, literature, music, politics, was a spectacle of dress, style, humor, sophistication, and black chic.

The CBC, in an attempt to emphasize its links with the black mayors around the country, had invited Tom Bradley of Los Angeles to speak. Bradley symbolized the new political power of blacks in the city halls — Detroit, Los Angeles, Newark, Washington, D.C., Atlanta, Gary, and dozens of others. Black mayors, unlike black congressmen, controlled patronage, judgeships, the poverty programs, the disbursement of federal grants, and similar administrative powers. The other principal speaker was Senator Edward Brooke, whose presence was clearly a CBC signal that it would seek alliances with Republicans and any others who might further black interests.

The CBC thereafter took very practical steps to broaden its appeal and organize its resources. The new, postelection chairman, Congressman Louis Stokes of Ohio, quite deliberately deflated black expectations on CBC and limited the caucus only to those activities it could best handle — legislative research and proposals. He discarded CBC's various roles as national black spokesman, investigative body, and clearinghouse; he tightened its belt and strengthened the research staff. This, he said, converted the CBC into a "legitimate power pocket," which could negotiate realistically with whites on legislation.[34]

Then the members of the CBC began to make more effective use of their growing seniority than ever before. Congressman Diggs, the first chairman of CBC, became in 1973 the first black chairman of the Committee on the District of Columbia. He immediately used his position to vote out the first home rule bill for the District in 102 years. Other CBC members resorted to the old white game of political "hardball" when alliances or seniority didn't work. Before the District of Columbia bill came up for a House vote, Delegate Fauntroy leaked a memorandum to the press that named the congressional districts in which the black "swing vote" might be turned in the next election against white congressmen who opposed the measure. The analysis suggested that blacks now had "considerable political influence in determining the outcome of races in 86 congressional districts" in two ways: first, because in fifty-eight of the congressional districts (thirty-seven of them in the South), blacks made up 25 percent or more of the population; second, because in fifty-one of the congressional districts, blacks of voting age represented roughly two or more times the margin of victory of the winning candi-

date in 1972.[35] The memo created an uproar and one congressman attacked it as a "clumsy political ploy," but a home rule
bill finally passed, suggesting that the flexing of black muscles
did not hurt and would remain a feature of Congress.[36]

Finally, the whirlwind of race — still hovering over the
American landscape — was winding down, at least temporarily,
because of President Nixon's own colossal misjudgments,
rather than as a result of the CBC's appeals to coalitions.
Nixon's massive assaults on progressive programs in early 1973
made the issue of economic survival no longer a racial one but
a class one, uniting poor blacks and poor whites. And Watergate so irreversibly damaged Nixon that it seemed to redress
the imbalance created by his so-called mandate against minorities. By the end of 1973, indeed, George Wallace thought it
politically wise in his own state of Alabama, 26 percent black,
to address the Southern Conference of Black Mayors where,
improbably, he received a standing ovation; and, in 1975, he
appointed a black to his cabinet. And when Gerald Ford
assumed the presidency in August 1974, he met immediately
with the CBC to show his concern about the nation's blacks.

The modest success of the CBC in the early seventies
rapidly repeated itself at all levels of American society. Black
caucuses popped up in the Democratic National Committee;
in some eighteen state legislatures; in the influential National
League of Cities (as the National Black Caucus of Local
Elected Officials), which represents over 15,000 municipalities
and which elected as its own president, in the early seventies,
black Mayor Tom Bradley; in the AFL-CIO as the Coalition
of Black Trade Unionists (CBTU); in the South (where 20
percent of the population is black) as the Voter Registration
Project, which registered over one million blacks in the eleven

states of the Old Confederacy from 1966 to 1973; and as the Southern Elections Fund, which gave campaign assistance to local blacks to help increase the number of black elected officials in the region from 72 to 1555 over the period of 1965 to 1974.

During the later seventies, the CBC's role began to enlarge, but only as black activity in the nation spread. The executive director of the CBC until 1974, Augustus Alven Adair, a talented man with a Ph.D. in political science from Johns Hopkins, quite candidly admitted that

> while the CBC does have the power to mobilize support for legislation within Congress and we can give technical advice to outside black groups, such as Jesse Jackson's Operation PUSH, still we cannot replace the existing civil rights organizations like the NAACP, PUSH, SCLC, NWRO, et cetera, or the black mayors and state leaders. They are still around. They can do things which we simply can't do — like arousing and organizing outside groups around issues, setting up lobbies in states and cities for blacks, acting as an ombudsman for minority interests.[37]

A powerful alliance of convenience between the CBC and these independent black movements was forming, leading to de facto black coalitions in Congress, in cities and in state legislatures. Some sharp-sighted realists observed these new developments as indications of a kind of "big bang" theory of black involvement in American politics in the 1970s.

I talked with Robert Maynard, the brilliant, young black journalist on the Washington *Post*, who had covered the early years of the CBC for his newspaper. His interpretation of the converging black movements was bullish.

> The CBC's activities have set in motion all sorts of new possibilities for black politics. Right now blacks in combination might

be able to choose the next presidential nominee in the Democratic Party. In nineteen seventy-six, many of the black representatives in the CBC will be in their fifth terms. The most important black mayors, like Bradley of Los Angeles, Hatcher of Gary, Young of Detroit, Jackson of Atlanta, Gibson of Newark, will have powerful political organizations in their cities. Most blacks will still live in the most important states of the North and Southeast, where their voting prowess is magnified by the electoral system of presidential voting. Furthermore, the CBTU will be a vital force among labor unions. Put all that together with the several thousand local elected officials, add in the independent organizations like PUSH, and you have one hell of a force. The only missing ingredient is someone to be a unifying vision for the black movement.[38]

Such sentiments have become de minimis among black strategists. The tantalizing question, however, remains: can groups like the CBC ever overcome the white voter's fear of race? Can CBC neutralize or by-pass the profound anxieties that candidates like Wallace stir up in the electorate? A solution may be possible only through emphasis on other issues — primarily, according to political analyst Samuel Lubell, economic ones — or through the emergence of a liberal leader with the vision of a Robert Kennedy.

Over twenty million black voters, nonetheless, will still figure importantly in the victories of many liberal candidates. And blacks are now reasoning, Why should we not translate our liberal electoral strength into bargaining chips in both parties? In 1972, most black "pressure" tactics failed, but in 1976, black organizations, in particular the CBC and its local black allies, will be more seasoned and far more aggressive in their designs on power. This means there will be more willingness to obtain and enforce black unity. The CBC, with its unique national status, may be the organization to lead that new racial bloc.

However that issue is resolved, the CBC's exalted station remains self-evident. As long as blacks in the House are virtually the only blacks to function and serve in national offices, then the CBC will inevitably be in the vanguard of the country's blacks. The role of the CBC may diminish as more blacks win mayoralty elections — which they are doing at an accelerated clip — or Senate seats, or as they gain new appointments to the federal government. But for the moment, in this decade, the CBC serves the day-to-day interests of black reformers as a forum for raising issues, sparking debates, and drawing up agenda of social change for a national audience. Always more powerful as a moral than an electoral force, the CBC remains the mouth through which the roar of a people can be heard.

4 ☆

The Unions Divide

FOR YEARS, the labor movement subsidized liberal reform politics in America. Labor contributed heavily to the Americans For Democratic Action upon its founding in 1947. Unions purchased thousands of subscriptions to the Democratic Party's newsletter of the 1950s, *The Democratic Digest*, when the party was in debt. Many unions supported the research activities of liberal representatives in Congress through the Democratic Study Group in the House. Through the sixties, unions funded, gave office space to, and supplied personnel for progressive groups in Washington that were fighting for New Frontier–Great Society programs, for national health insurance, and tax reform.

When *The New Democrat* was first published, it seemed that the unions would be natural allies to turn to for financial support. We couldn't have been more mistaken, however. By the 1970s, the labor unions were unnatural kin. Most of them were not the same organizations they had been in the 1930s and early 1960s; or, more precisely, they *were* the same organizations they had been in those two decades — it was just that the times had overtaken them.

Much of the leadership had grown old and conservative by the elections of 1968. Under the autocratic and cranky George Meany, for example, most AFL-CIO unions in the late sixties favored the Vietnam War, opposed the antiwar campaigns of Senators Kennedy, McCarthy and McGovern, dropped out of the ADA because of its 1968 endorsement of McCarthy, helped broker Hubert Humphrey's nomination, championed the hard-hats against the youth, and listened in worshipful silence to Meany's denunciations of the New Politics in the seventies — one of his typical comments, pronounced in mid-1970, that the Democratic Party "almost has got to be the party of the extremists insofar as those so-called liberals or new lefts, or whatever you want to call them, have taken [it] over."[1] In short, many once friendly unions, now informally led by George Meany, distrusted intellectuals, feminists, militant black politicians, and others of the new workers for change.

This faction of labor reserved a special venom for the Democratic Party reformers. The party reforms, which we so lustily promoted in *The New Democrat*, were, in the eyes of Meany's minions, infernal devices designed to blow the traditional labor influence off the landscape. From the start, Meany summarily ordered COPE, led by his ardent disciple, Alexander E. Barkan, to boycott the McGovern Commission hearings.

Later, when the reforms didn't vanish, Meany attempted to pack the reform commissions with his own party regulars. He unleashed COPE on the New Politicians who tried to get posts on the commissions, leading to one famous scrap in which liberal Senator Harold Hughes was thrust aside in favor of a COPE ally, Patricia Harris, as temporary head of the Democratic Credentials Committee (which was to review the states' compliance with party rules at the 1972 convention). This heavy-handed intervention left a residue of bitterness among liberals and moderates. When everything else failed, Meany tried to use the reforms to win delegates for labor; he ordered COPE to piece together some uncommitted "labor slates" to run in delegate elections. But his involvement was too little and too late — his troops went down to bitter defeat in the 1972 primaries.

All of us at *The New Democrat* shared a profound personal distrust of men like George Meany. We felt that Meany and other labor leaders had been too facile in their sweeping condemnation of antiwar protesters over the years. They seemed to take for granted that most of labor was prowar, even though Gallup polls in 1970 showed union members split over the war in about the same proportions as all of American society. Still, the war issue did not stop Meany and his allies from lavishing millions of dollars of union funds on the re-election campaigns of dovish congressional and senatorial Democrats in 1968, 1970, and 1972 (including McGovern in 1968 and 1974). Even Meany and his friends wanted a pro-union Congress more than a vote against communism and Chinese Reds and "totalitarianism."

There were, though, a few maverick groups in the labor union ranks to which we could turn in the late sixties; their members espoused liberal policies, opposed the war and Lyndon Johnson, and lauded the party reforms. Best known was the United Auto Workers (UAW), which had quit the AFL-CIO in 1968 because its late, strong-willed leader, Walter Reuther, couldn't stomach the callous indifference that George Meany showed toward new unionization, Southeast Asia, and other social issues. Indeed, the UAW, long in advance of the reform movements, had already elected a few women and blacks to positions of responsibility.

A number of other unions that, unlike the UAW, were still within the AFL-CIO ranks, were also sympathetic to our progressive ideas. The largest of these were the Communications Workers of America (CWA), whose leader, Joseph Beirne, had strongly favored the Vietnam War in 1968 but who had subsequently broken with Meany; the International Association of Machinists (IAM); and the American Federation of State, County and Municipal Employees (AFSCME). These unions, along with the UAW, played an independent and active role in the movement that most concerned progressives in the Democratic Party — the reform crusade. They sent their officials to testify in favor of the guidelines at the McGovern Commission hearings; they proselytized for the changes at union meetings; they alerted their local chapters to the delegate elections; and they applied heavy pressure on state parties to comply with the commission's recommendations. As a result of their energetic activity, the reforms began to work and they began to elect many of their members as delegates in 1972.

In the summer of 1970, I visited the United Auto Workers and their Washington representative, Bill Dodds. Dodds was one of the authentically progressive war-horses of the labor movement. A small, hyperactive, sharp-tongued idealist, he ran a vigorous Washington office and championed reform causes, heedless of the outrage he might kick up among Meany loyalists.

Dodds was sympathetic to *The New Democrat*'s plight and suggested several aids for increasing our circulation, including a mention of the magazine in the UAW journal, the possibility that the UAW might buy 100 or more subscriptions at ten dollars apiece, and the scheduling of some meetings with other labor people at local chapters. As a consequence of Dodds' intervention, the UAW newsletter did give some play to *The New Democrat*, which proved helpful, and Dodds put together some useful conferences for us with men and women in the trade union movement. However, because of the UAW's depleted strike fund, in hazardous shape just as the UAW was heading into its negotiations with the "big three" auto companies, the union never bought block subscriptions to *The New Democrat* for their members.

Through a friend, I got in touch with another union, the United Steelworkers. Its Washington representative, James O'Brien, was a lively Irishman with a touch of the leprechaun. He had special compassion for underdogs and was full of sympathy for the reformers. He had supported Robert Kennedy in 1968 over objections from his bosses in the union; in the 1970s, he had defended the students, the women, and the blacks; and he took an absorbing interest in practically any humanitarian crusade that came his way.

O'Brien agreed to prod his union into purchasing block subscriptions to *The New Democrat*. And a few months later, the Steelworkers purchased 100 subscriptions a month, thereby keeping us alive for a fateful period when we were beginning our coverage of the reforms, and just as the guidelines were being implemented in the states. The Steelworkers' bosses, however, since they were fundamentally prowar and pro-Meany, soon got exasperated with the arrangement and terminated it.

For the most part, in the early seventies, my visits to the unions were unproductive. Most union leaders, even progressive ones, shied away from any aggressively liberal causes (including the antiwar and women's movements) that might

85

threaten their relations with the AFL-CIO hierarchy. They apparently figured there was no point starting a quarrel with the AFL-CIO over minor matters when they needed the help of conservative unions on issues basic to survival, such as defending the sanctity of the union shop, warding off threats to the movement like the right-to-work laws, fighting together for increases in the minimum wage and social security, and sponsoring joint legislation for programs like federally subsidized medical care. While they might accept a description of some unions as liberal and others as conservative, they felt that the few spats over issues did not mar basic labor consensus and were not a signal of a fundamental break-up in union politics. They had an abiding belief in the solidarity of the federation.

Indeed, Michael Harrington, a booster of Robert Kennedy in 1968, a realist on liberal politics, then head of the late Norman Thomas Socialist Party, and hardly a fan of George Meany's, wrote in 1970 of the AFL-CIO:

> In three conventions during the Sixties, the AFL-CIO adopted a sweeping program which goes far beyond anything proposed in the days of Franklin Roosevelt and is specific about how to reconstruct this society in a way the intellectuals might emulate. At the 1963 convention, the AFL-CIO endorsed national economic planning; in 1965, there was another proposal for a national planning agency and advocacy of a massive commitment to rebuild the cities and a peacetime GI bill; and in 1967, George Meany told the delegates that "increasingly the problems of our members . . . are not so much problems of the work place itself, but problems of environment and problems of living and raising a family in today's complex, crowded, urbanized, and suburbanized society."[2]

In 1972, I might add, at election time, the federation advocated wiping out $20 billion in tax shelters for corporations, including capital gains and the oil depletion allowance; expanding day-care centers; and enacting national health insurance and minimum family assistance. Next year, the federation, after much hemming and hawing, finally endorsed the Equal Rights Amendment for women. George Meany also actively embraced Cesar Chavez's troubled farmworkers union and backed the Chicanos who were striking the Farah plant in El Paso, Texas.

In 1972, these few liberal emblems on the AFL-CIO's record kept reformist unions, now militantly antiwar and hostile to Nixon and mistrustful of the Meany unions, from breaking completely with Meany and going sharply to the left during the primaries. Thus, while *The New Democrat* was plugging away for McGovern, we were not greatly surprised to see that most of our friendly liberal unions were sticking close to a politically respectable position and endorsing Senator Muskie for the Democratic nomination. Leonard Woodcock of the UAW, and Jerry Wurf of the AFSCME openly supported Muskie, and even George Meany acknowledged privately that he could live with a Muskie nomination.

But the McGovern triumph changed all that. For the first time, a profound chasm opened publicly within trade union ranks that surprised everyone in labor. The politics of the labor movement through one catharsis caught up to its practical realities. Wurf and Woodcock angrily parted ways with Meany to endorse McGovern — indeed, many liberal unions came out in the open for the first time as truly progressive political organizations. The conservative unions, in turn, coalesced as a large neutral bloc around Meany — a bloc that was largely responsible for the Nixon re-election victory.

Meany's decision to go neutral on McGovern was, of course,

not surprising. Meany openly mistrusted McGovern's positions on Russia and China, defense, trade, and other issues. He often said that McGovern's supporters showed "contempt" for the workingman and "naiveté" about communism, and propounded "reckless" programs for defense cutbacks and "elitism" in their ideas for governing the country. His preferences were for men like Lyndon Johnson, Hubert Humphrey, or Henry Jackson — though, in 1971, he remarked indiscreetly that he could tolerate any Democrat except John Lindsay.

The lack of personal rapport between Meany and McGovern further compounded their differences. Meany's animus against McGovern stemmed partly from the latter's race for the presidency in 1968, partly from McGovern's personal lack of deference to Meany, partly from a series of misunderstandings and slights, real and imagined, between the two men. McGovern held in silence his own deep reservations about Meany.

More importantly, during the 1968 Humphrey campaign, Meany's COPE had stage-managed, funded, deployed the field operations, and set up the media advertising for the Humphrey operation. Now, under the new reforms, a rude shock had occurred: McGovern had been able to slip by the labor brass and into the Democratic Party nomination without getting assistance from the AFL-CIO or receiving its blessing. Thereby McGovern had radically diminished the power of the federation in the party.

Jerry Wurf understood this event to be the actual basis of Meany's angry neutrality resolution. In a piece he wrote for *The New Republic* (shortly after he had attended the federation conference and unsuccessfully urged a McGovern endorsement), Wurf asserted that the Executive Council vote had more to do with how McGovern won the nomination than with his record before or during the campaign. Since 1948 the unions had nearly always been a major force in the selection of the Democratic nominees and the formulation of the party's platform and campaign strategy. The assumption was that, Chicago and the party reforms notwithstanding, it would be that way in 1972 . . . But George Meany and the AFL-CIO leadership did not participate — although participation was solicited — in the drawing up of the rules for state and national party reform . . . As a consequence, AFL-CIO leaders and staff found themselves ill-prepared, in early 1972, to cope with what was happening. Labor divided in some states and stayed "uncommitted" in others, but in neither case could the COPE leaders head off the momentum of reform . . . the real concern was participation and access, the AFL-CIO's vested interest which ignored the rich opportunities for workers and their unions in the more open, "new" party.[3]

Even Lane Kirkland, secretary-treasurer of the AFL-CIO, admitted to the same reasoning after the 1972 election. "As a rule," he said, "we haven't made an effort to put 'labor' delegates on state delegations. We haven't had to, because the party structure in the past was won by professional politicians. And they would consult us. We could be pretty sure that whatever came out of the process wouldn't be too offensive to us . . . We were aware of the McGovern reforms, but the 'quota' business took us by surprise. And we didn't get serious enough about the state conventions until it was too late. McGovern really won the nomination in those conventions."[4]

The union's hostility to the reforms was the source of some amusement to historians. As Arthur M. Schlesinger, Jr., remarked: "It is especially diverting that the trade unionists, who so outraged the Democratic establishment when they forced their way into the party under the New Deal, have now become such fervent members of the party establishment themselves that they cannot abide the sight of new and unfamiliar faces following their own example thirty years before. Blood transfusions can be painful."[5]

Ironically, despite Meany's trepidations there were far more labor union members as delegates at the Miami convention than in 1968. Most, however, were from the progressive unions, or they were rank and filers, but they were not leaders. Men of influence in previous conventions, like Al Barkan of COPE and George Meany, were on the sidelines; they had no votes. Whatever authority they exercised was negative, through confrontations like the unsuccessful California challenge. Bob Keefe, the political consultant to the AFL-CIO in 1971–72, reflected the sentiments of the disgruntled union chieftains when he said, "Labor had more delegates and less influence than ever before."[6]

Meany at the time attempted weakly to pass off his opposition to McGovern on grounds other than the reforms or ideology. At the meeting at which the AFL-CIO voted twenty-seven to three to go neutral, Meany uttered all sorts of unproven allegations against the nominee, including a charge that McGovern had once double-crossed labor by voting against the repeal of Section 14(b) of the Taft-Hartley Act, which permits state right-to-work laws that weaken union security — this despite the fact that McGovern's voting record was almost straight prolabor compared to Nixon's unashamedly antiunion history. Other Meany apologists later tried to justify the master's behavior as a maneuver to preserve his leadership in an AFL-CIO stacked with pro-Nixon building trade unions and to keep a sensible line of communication open to the new Republican administration which, according to the polls, was going to return to power in a landslide. But this did little to explain away why Meany turned his back on the only union sympathizer in the race. The reasons were inextricably embedded in the snarls and tangles of ideology and reform and the war — along with the monumental clash of personality that divided McGovern and Meany from the beginning.

The press coverage of Meany's decision was extraordinary. Without a modicum of analysis, the media simply concluded that all unions had turned against McGovern. In reading the news accounts of the period, I did not at first realize, even from within the campaign, that many federation unions — as well as those outside the AFL-CIO — had not followed Meany's edict. Many had, in fact, broken publicly with Meany over the neutrality resolution and had endorsed McGovern. The news, however, only gradually seeped through to the public (and to me); but a genuine and widespread rebellion had erupted in union ranks, an act unprecedented in scope and with earthshaking implications for the future of the labor movement.

Within weeks, half the members of the AFL-CIO Executive Board repudiated the neutrality resolution and, in their capacity as leaders of individual unions, endorsed McGovern. By the end of August 1972, 33 of the 110 AFL-CIO constituent unions, plus some Steelworkers locals, publicly backed McGovern. Two unions outside the federation, the United Auto Workers, and the officers and many locals of the National Education Association (NEA), and even a few Teamsters locals followed suit. Paul Wieck summed up the implications in *The New Republic*: these unions "not only have a clear majority of all AFL-CIO members (over 7 million persons), but, with the single exception of the United Steelworkers, include all the major unions that traditionally have given a lot of money and manpower to campaigns."[7]

Some of the most courageous unions took dramatic steps to register their protest against the AFL-CIO neutrality by withdrawing their contributions to COPE. The four largest COPE dropouts were the Amalgamated Meatcutters (550,000 members), the American Federation of State, County and Municipal Employees (612,000 members), the Communications Workers of America (550,000 members), and the International Association of Machinists (927,000 members). These unions had, in the past, each given in the range of $120,000 annually. Their withdrawal, except from COPE's voter-registration programs, partially crippled COPE's operation.

To understand how serious a blow-up this was, it is instructive to note how many new alliances, independent of the AFL-CIO, were sealed, and how many fresh, autonomous political committees popped up to replace the discredited COPE operation. For example, AFSCME created its own political contributions union called PEOPLE (Public Employees Organized to Promote Legislative Equality), which raised $150,000 in 1972 and began to train its members as technicians for state and local campaigns. AFSCME also decided to work with the mammoth non-AFL-CIO teachers union, the National Education Association (1.2 million members), and with the National Treasury Employees Union, through a loose organization called the Coalition of American Public Employees (CAPE). CWA set up ten independent, regional directorships, in addition to committees in each state where CWA had members. In 1973, CWA allied itself with two other pro-McGovern unions, the Retail Clerks (558,000 members) and the Graphic Arts Union (130,000 members), to undertake joint political activities. The Machinists considered merging with the UAW and its Community Action Programs (CAP) in a 1973 joint conference in Washington, though no formal bargain was struck. Other unions outside the federation, like the UAW (205,000 members), established separate political fund-raising kitties. The UMW reactivated its Non-Partisan League as COMPAC (Coal Miners' Political Action Committee), which had become inactive after Tony Boyle, the former UAW president, was indicted for giving illegal campaign contributions in 1968.

Even the blacks within the AFL-CIO organized a new coalition — the Coalition of Black Trade Unionists (CBTU) described in Chapter 3. Bill Lucy, Secretary-Treasurer of AFSCME, one of the most innovative young blacks in labor's ranks, later explained that the CBTU was "formed out of the frustration that came from the Executive Council of the AFL-CIO assuming a neutrality position on the question of McGovern versus Nixon, which was absolutely in opposition to the desires of black workers and the black community."[8] The CBTU blossomed into a serious force, attracting some thirty-three unions, representing over one million black workers.

The McGovern tempest, then, marked the beginning of a new stage in labor politics. The break-away unions — CWA, the Retail Clerks, AFSCME, Graphic Arts, Oil, Chemical and Atomic Workers, International Union of Electricians, UAW, IAM, and the CBTU — contained about five million out of the twenty million union rank and file in the country. (This does not include the other less political unions that endorsed

McGovern.) Out of the McGovern controversy, a new movement emerged in American labor to challenge the old family politics of George Meany. As Paul Wieck observed, "The result, to quote one labor leader, is to 'bring to the forefront a whole new generation of labor leaders while the entrenched, aging leadership sits on the sidelines of the presidential campaign.' "[9]

Who were these new rebellious leaders? Who were the men and women who repudiated the Meany tradition of enforcing a joint political stance for all the unions?

Shortly after the election, I talked with several. First was Floyd Smith, a large, bluff man who heads the International Association of Machinists, a union buffeted in recent years by waves of blacks, women, and Chicanos demanding greater representation on its ruling boards. Smith took some pains to describe his decision as a relatively uncomplicated one, though clearly he was heeding the demands of his restless membership. He had endorsed McGovern, he asserted, because "McGovern believed in the things we believed in for the workingman. He had a pretty fair voting record as far as the labor movement was concerned. Nixon was always conservative." Though Smith regarded IAM's breach with Meany as temporary, he insisted IAM would not give money to COPE again, and he criticized COPE for calling him a "far-out liberal."[10] All the time he spoke, he radiated the impression of a man (with a union) who was savoring a new-found political independence.

Jerry Wurf, the vibrant, sparkling iconoclast who runs the AFSCME, probably the most rapidly expanding union in the seventies, was unabashedly profane in spelling out his reasons for AFSCME's break with the AFL-CIO's neutrality. He

94

blamed COPE's "mistakes" for his precipitous withdrawal. COPE and its allies had made a "basic error by not involving themselves in the work of the reform commissions. Then COPE took positions in the nineteen seventy-two primaries for Humphrey and Jackson or uncommitted slates without consulting us despite the fact that they were using our funds. Then at Miami, I was distressed that COPE was croaking McGovern unilaterally after he had fairly won the Democratic nomination. I thought we should let all the AFL-CIO unions decide for themselves on the presidential endorsement."[11]

This assessment was fiercely endorsed by Victor Gotbaum, a dark, shaggy, articulate man, one of Wurf's principal lieutenants, who heads the influential New York local of AFSCME. He declared flatly that "Meany today is a lion who is roaring but nobody is listening . . . He promotes a myth of labor solidarity. But today we are a movement of movements."[12]

The late Joseph Beirne, the peppery, acid-tongued chief of the CWA, insisted bluntly, too, that:

I withdrew from COPE because it was out of touch with what was happening in the political process — with the reforms which I think were a natural evolution in the Democratic Party, and with McGovern who was the candidate who had done the most for the working man. COPE must be changed. We who contribute to it have no control over it or participation in its policy decisions. The COPE leaders live in the dreams of the past, where they wheeled and dealed in politics. The Executive Council of the AFL-CIO should be reformed, too. All we do there is endorse candidates and nothing else. Our union now feels we can make our own political decisions and spend our money more fruitfully by going it alone.[13]

Besides Floyd Smith, Jerry Wurf, and Joseph Beirne, there was an odd assortment of other leaders who, for a variety of reasons, broke publicly with Meany — and COPE — over the neutrality resolution. The sentiment that these men shared in common, which emerged again and again during my interviews with them, was a conviction that the AFL-CIO no longer had its finger on the pulse of progressive politics in the nation. Most seemed genuinely angered by the obtuseness of the COPE operation and the small-mindedness of George Meany.

Curiously, the members of these unions were not always as liberal as their leaders. The most progressive unions were the UAW and the AFSCME. The bulk of the UAW and the AFSCME predictably favored McGovern because of a tradition of able, socially conscious leaders, and a large number of blacks and women, who were generally progressive (although the UAW also had white locals who voted for Wallace in 1968 and would have backed him in 1972 if he had run). And later the UMW insurgents who in December 1972 ousted their corrupt president, Tony Boyle, in a bloody campaign, helped create an enormously knowledgeable and reform-minded cadre of miners and leaders.

Other unions endorsing McGovern, however, were progressive more because of the character of the individual who sat in the President's office than because of pressure from their members. In this category were unions like the Oil, Chemical and Atomic Workers (OCAW), led by Al Grospiron; the Amalgamated Meatcutters, run by Patrick Gorman; and the American Federation of Teachers (AFT), headed for a time by David Selden until, in 1974, the Meany-backed conservative, Albert Shanker, toppled him.

The Unions Divide

Some unions endorsed McGovern for more esoteric reasons. The mercurial Joseph Beirne of the CWA was a hawk in 1968 and resigned from the ADA in protest against its endorsement of Eugene McCarthy, but in 1969 he suddenly began to promote the party reforms at the McGovern hearings, and in 1972 he parted company with Meany over neutrality and privately expressed contempt for the old warrior. (In 1974, a like-minded lieutenant, Glenn E. Watts, succeeded Beirne as CWA president. Beirne died later the same year.)

What impact the sensational labor break-away had on the McGovern campaign was sometimes unclear. When I first arrived in the campaign in June 1972, only one staff man was assigned to labor and he wasn't taken very seriously as McGovern's envoy to the unions — either by the campaign or by labor. Bill Dodds, the UAW representative, quietly helped the McGovern people on the side. However, after the neutrality resolution passed the AFL-CIO, the pro-McGovern unions hastily patched together a McGovern-Shriver Labor Committee. They donated approximately $250,000. Many unions set up adjacent offices at local and state McGovern headquarters. Robert Keefe, a former consultant to George Meany, later campaign manager for Birch Bayh's abortive presidential effort, and no McGovern zealot, commented that "the unions that jumped in and supported George McGovern did so quite wholeheartedly and gave a best-effort kind of thing. It was a broad range of unions, certainly far beyond the number of unions that had supported Senator McGovern in the primaries or at the convention. The Textile Workers, for example, had been very strongly anti-McGovern, but in the fall campaign they did everything within their power to support the Democratic ticket."[14]

The true grit of this new alliance, however, was tested in light of the disaster of the 1972 election, which saw Nixon's support almost double among union families, from 29 percent in 1968 to 54 percent in 1972. Many of the pro-McGovern union leaders I spoke to were plainly shocked by the rout. Yet none of them felt he had erred in his endorsement of Mc-govern. As a group, they believed he was defeated on personal grounds, not on ideological ones. McGovern's collapse only strengthened their determination to keep alive their progressive politics within the labor movement.

These same unions ostentatiously began to signal a post-election independence from Meany. Many of them bought tables at an ADA dinner honoring the new president of the UMW, Arnold Miller, after his upset victory over the Meany loyalist, Tony Boyle, while the Meany claque stayed away. A convocation of the Congressional Black Caucus engendered a similar split in attendance among AFL-CIO unions.

However, given the appearance of two separate wings of labor within the Democratic Party, most of the factional interest in labor circles began to devolve on the body whose power mattered — the Democratic National Committee — and pitched battles began to shake the insides of the committees. In one corner, weighing in for George Meany and waving the pennant of "regularity," was the campaign-toughened COPE organization. Al Barkan, whom even his friends have described as "more holy than the Pope," set about rooting out the New Politics "crazies" (as he often called them) with the same zeal the old unionists had used to purge communists from their ranks in the thirties and forties.

In the other corner were unions like the CWA, the IAM, AFSCME, the UAW, Graphic Arts, and a few smaller unions, which banded together as an informal but highly disciplined caucus in the party to fight COPE and protect the reforms. The liberals were helped for a short time at the DNC by McGovern's control of the committee. His party leader, Jean Westwood, appointed at least a dozen progressive laborites to crucial posts on the national committee and the party's two reform commissions before McGovern departed in November.

Barkan's offensive against the liberal unions began, unlike most "family" fights within labor, with public statements of outrage and pain issued in the newspapers and magazines and over television. Barkan, a reclusive fixer, permitted private words to leak to favorite columnists. He threatened a COPE war and stated behind closed doors that "the reforms must be wiped out." He unleashed for public consumption his pet intellectual, Albert Shanker of the AFT, who warned at Democratic Party forums that the New Politics liberals had "contempt" for workers' values, a "dilettantish approach to economic problems, reverse racism, and anti-American foreign policy."[15]

The progressives retorted in kind, with maximum effect. Feisty Bill Dodds, a proponent of the involvement of reform unions in party politics to counterbalance COPE, told the *Washington Post*: "To me, it seems dangerous for one segment of the labor movement to be as involved in one party as Barkan and COPE are today. There is no precedent for this. In a day and age when you're trying to keep political structures open to the public, it leaves you open to retribution from those who are not sympathetic to labor."[16] Victor Gotbaum of AFSCME, a member of the Mikulski Commission, condemned the histrionics of labor men "who deserted the party the last time around and then try to tell us what to do."[17]

99

The battle between the two labor wings started in earnest in December 1972 — not a month after the election — with the selection of Texan Robert Strauss, the COPE candidate, as Democratic National Committee chairman. The liberal coalition's candidate lost by a slim margin. Then, in March 1973, COPE tried to name members for all eight slots allocated to labor in the twenty-five at-large seats for the DNC; its eight nominees included only one who had supported Mc-Govern in 1972. Floyd Smith and Joseph Beirne threatened full-scale war unless Strauss added their names to the slate; he did so, angering Barkan. The progressive unions defeated COPE in the spring of 1973 on the selection of chairman of the Democratic State Chairmen's Association. In the summer, they won again in choosing the president of the Young Democrats.

The progressive unions scored their most significant triumph over COPE in 1974, however, when the Democratic Party reforms were essentially retained through the Mikulski compromise. Even COPE's former ally, Robert Strauss, eventually accepted this plan. COPE denounced the agreement and planned to fight it all the way to the 1976 convention. However, COPE's first counteroffensive, at the National Committee meeting in 1974, was supported by only a handful of voters and its second rear-guard action at the 1974 mid-term convention sank out of sight without a murmur.

Indeed, by the mid-1970s, even COPE's advocates in the AFL-CIO were responding more to the attitudes of the progressive caucuses than to the bellows of Al Barkan. The momentous questions of inflation, recession, and of the impeachment of President Nixon momentarily brought together the two factions in a loose "labor front" against the very man who had originally disrupted the labor movement in 1972. Meany's scorn was now turned fully on the President, and the liberal unions were more sure than ever that they had been right in backing McGovern in 1972. Their resolve to remain independent of the AFL-CIO politics in the future increased. In fact, David Broder noted in a long analysis he made of the labor split in 1973 that "Beirne, Smith and Wurf, in particular, have been reluctant to close ranks with Meany and Barkan since the election, and all three men are aggressively building their own unions' political arms."[18]

One theme I noticed in my interviews repeated itself again and again — the enthusiasm among progressive labor leaders about the future of their independent political movement. They tended to regard it as part of a larger historical evolution within labor. They subscribed to the sentiments of David Selden, former head of the AFT, who predicted: "The liberal movement will grow stronger in the unions. You look back a few years ago to nineteen seventy-two. The union movement was totally conservative. The war and the McGovern campaign brought liberals out of the closet. Dissent within the labor movement today is tempting even more people to break away from the old doctrines."[19]

What was carrying the split relentlessly forward was the new trend of union membership in the 1960s and 1970s. The formation of the CBTU in 1972, for example, was a public acknowledgment of one of the swiftest new currents flowing through labor — the increasing black make-up of unions, which was gradually eating away the Irish-Catholic, white base of old-line labor.

Few unionists recognized the magnitude of this development. By 1973, one-third of the total black work force held union cards. Blacks amounted to 500,000 out of the 1.5 million members of the UAW; 200,000 of the 1.8 million in the Steelworkers; 180,000 out of the 612,000 in the AFSCME. They were a large percentage of the workers in the hospital unions, in many service-related trades, and in other industrial unions.[20] Clearly, it was no simple coincidence that the unions with large black populations — excluding the more conservative Steelworkers, who faced legions of rebellious blacks because of their "stand-still" policies — were the most outspoken reformers in labor. Reports issued by the Bureau of Labor Statistics suggested further that in the seventies blacks were more likely to join unions in proportion to their presence in the work force than whites.[21] This meant that as long as union membership remained static, as it had in the AFL-CIO for two decades since the 1955 merger — at about fifteen million — black membership was likely to rise proportionately more quickly than white membership.

The flow of black labor into unions, indeed, seemed virtually unchecked except at one bottleneck — the building trades. Craft rules perennially managed to exclude black workers (and Puerto Ricans) from construction work. Blacks, for instance, in New York City Building Trades, were 1.5 percent in 1960 and only 2 percent in 1970.[22] The issue of racial exclusion was gradually splitting labor into integrated and segregated unions and heating up yet another source of conflict between the progressive caucus and the unions affiliated with COPE, many of which were construction unions.

After one year of existence, the CBTU was itself acting as a liberal counterweight to the status quo policies of the AFL-CIO. For example, it opposed George Meany over the appointment of Peter Brennan, a construction union leader in

New York state, as Nixon's secretary of labor (Meany himself later turned against Brennan); over revenue sharing (the CBTU favored it because poor blacks were the victims of most decaying cities; Meany opposed it for lack of federal controls over the money); and over the affirmative-action programs in the Democratic Party delegate selection (the CBTU approved of affirmative action with compliance monitored by the party; the AFL-CIO opposed anything that remotely resembled quotas, including most forms of affirmative action). Bill Lucy conceded that, because of these wrangles, many labor people "accused the Coalition of being separatist, anti-AFL-CIO, antagonistic, a protest movement. But we never had a quarrel with the AFL-CIO. We just felt that blacks should have some input into decisions."[23] The Coalition did stand side by side with Meany on some issues — for example, the controversial Burke-Hartke trade bill limiting certain foreign imports to protect American jobs.

Another trend shaking the labor movement was the growing number of women in the work force. In the early 1970s, the figure had risen to 4.5 million of the twenty million union members in the nation. In the spirit of the age, women were finally awakening to the fact that, though they sometimes — as in the needle trades — constituted a majority of the membership, they rarely had representation on union boards (in 1974, they made up 25 percent of the AFL-CIO and held fewer than 5 percent of the key posts), they were treated cavalierly on most decisions by labor, and some thirty-four million working women in the country were still unorganized.[24]

In March 1974, women trade unions organized to present their grievances. At the Chicago founding meeting of the Coalition of Labor Union Women (CLUW), Myra Wolfgang, vice-president of the Hotel and Restaurant Employees Union, threw down a gauntlet to the male chiefs, saying, "We have a message for George Meany. We have a message for Leonard Woodcock. We have a message for Frank Fitzsimmons. You can tell them we didn't come here to swap recipes."[25] Some 3000 women from fifty-eight labor unions roundly cheered.

Many CLUW women with whom I talked were determined that insensitive male officialdom would no longer dictate their political roles. Mildred Jeffrey, the astute UAW activist, explained to me that past excuses offered by men — that women are more interested in their homes and husbands than in union politics; that women don't seek or covet leadership; that women have special problems that prevent their doing a man's work — were no longer acceptable. Women were now adamant, she said, about casting out the hierarchies that barred them from leadership, especially in those unions where they made up most of the membership but held none of the offices. Women were determined, for instance, to have more than just two vice-presidencies in the liberal Amalgamated Clothing Workers since they constituted 80 percent of the employees.[26] The CLUW also intended to push for equal pay for equal work, affirmative action in hiring and promotion, and improved maternity benefits; in the political arena, they would fight for ratification of the Equal Rights Amendment, equal protective labor laws, and day-care legislation. The organizers of the CLUW went so far as to set up a labor caucus at the National Women's Political Caucus, so that blue-collar women could participate in the feminist politics of the coalition.

The self-assertion of the females and blacks in labor had the side effect of encouraging the trend toward union democracy, though this trend already had had its first dramatic expression in a predominantly white, male union. It happened in the UMW, when, in 1972, insurgent miners elected Arnold Miller as a liberal-reform president. This upheaval, brought about by angry, low-paid miners, many ill from lung disease and scarred by mining accidents, demonstrated that an aroused union membership could, with the help of the courts, the Department of Labor, and an internal rebellion, rid itself of villainous leadership and make itself progressive.

The trend toward democratic upheavals was intermittent and uncertain. Joseph Rauh, Jr., the tough civil rights lawyer who guided the legal challenges of the UMW through the courts, said in 1973 that liberals were wrong to rest their hopes for more progressive victories within organized labor on the thin reed of reform elections. He forecast a decline in insurgencies. "The reformers have lost two battles in the last few years, in the National Maritime Union, and in the Painters Union. I am very discouraged about the future of reform fights in the labor movement. I think the UMW might well be an exception."[27]

Surely the campaigns to overturn entrenched leaders were enormously complicated by the fact that some unions had become conglomerates, absorbing all varieties of unions into their folds in order to increase their dues and fortify their capacity to strike for long periods. The National Maritime Union, for example, originally organized to handle shipping, had expanded to include many unrelated industries. Maritime insurgents, therefore, found it hard, if not impossible, to arouse the sympathies of members from the unrelated trades, who had little acquaintance with the original union and didn't really care what happened to it.

Rauh was essentially correct in his caveat for yet another

reason — the unfortunate fact that liberal unions, in general, simply stayed out of the civil wars in brother unions even though the struggles might mean a new generation of progressive leaders. One observer suggested that this invisible charter could be traced back to the thirties, when unions felt they could not afford to fight among themselves because such quarrels would jeopardize their common struggle for survival against management. So even progressive leaders were ready in the 1970s to regard intervention in another's affairs as analogous to a family's calling in the cops when one of its children misbehaved.[28]

Thus, for instance, Floyd Smith reddened at my mention of UMW assistance to a number of union insurgents, and sputtered, "No union has the right to enter into a dispute concerning another labor union. I know the UMW tried to help the insurgents in the National Maritime Union election, but Arnold Miller showed inexperience when he gave aid to the reformers. No other union is doing what the UMW had done."[29] Even in the UMW's own internal fight, Rauh himself could not persuade Jerry Wurf of AFSCME to provide assistance because Wurf felt he could pick only so many quarrels with George Meany.[30] And though the UAW did hand over some money to the UMW crusaders, it did so surreptitiously. In short, the code of the unions dictated a non-intervention pact among brethren.

Nor, indeed, was democratization itself always a guarantee that progressivism would automatically burst forth. Even the new UMW in the early seventies was forced to reduce its investment in a broad range of liberal ideas associated with the mining industry because it had to adjust to the economic imperatives of its membership. Thus the new leadership abhorred strip mining, an anathema to liberals, but it had to face the fact that in the seventies more than one-half of all American coal would come from stripping. To survive as a union, the UMW had to organize strip miners, only 10 percent of whom were union members. Arnold Miller, as a result, supported a bill in Congress permitting stripping where restoration of the ravaged terrain was possible. Miller, like all responsible union leaders, looked out for his own men before he looked out for reform politics.[31]

The emergence of an independent liberal movement among unions in the seventies was a reality. But it was hampered by the economic necessities of survival, by the failure of fights for democracy within unions, and by lack of political maturity, until recently, among blacks, women, and other minorities. However, in line with the historical trends, most of these obstacles were gradually disintegrating.

One other reform upheaval with enormous implications for the labor movement may also be possible. A number of the large, autonomous unions, like the UAW, the UMW, and the NEA, are considering whether to rejoin (or, in the case of the NEA, join) the AFL-CIO, perhaps after Meany's departure. With their huge combined memberships added to the fast-flowing currents eddying around the traditional membership of labor, they might push the federation leftward. But this is still a far-off hope and might turn out to be a mirage. None of the three unions yet appears willing to pay the heavy dues demanded by the AFL-CIO. And their presence might be so jarring for the conservative unions as to prompt their secession from the federation.

The coalition of liberal unions in the mid-seventies nonetheless has now survived as a strong and lively movement by itself.

The progressive unions have ridden the swift political rapids of the McGovern debacle without losing their footing. They have almost 25 percent of the union members in the country, and that number is growing all the time. They have young leaders, and Meany's generation is dying off. They are at the forefront of free union elections, of the movements for equality of women, blacks, other minorities, and of the new issues.

A progressive labor movement is no longer, in short, a gleam in the eyes of a New Politics activist. It has been born; it has survived a rough childhood; it is now maturing into a young and forceful cause with increasing influence throughout American politics. Liberals, accustomed to the familiar brick wall of Meany and Barkan, now find an alternate route to reach workers — for votes, funds, and political support — through fraternal unions that share their beliefs and political ideals.

5 ☆

The Middle Class Meanders

WHITE, MIDDLE-CLASS LIBERALS, along with labor and the minorities, have traditionally dominated left-wing politics in the country. In the last twenty years, their influence has radiated through such organizations as the ADA and Citizens Organization for a Sane World (SANE), and their money has been dispensed to candidates through such intermediaries as the National Committee for an Effective Congress and the National Council for a Liveable World.

In 1968, anguished over the Vietnam War, many of these same liberals in academia, in the suburbs, in the cities, rose in rebellion against Lyndon Johnson in the Democratic primaries. At first, they had no organization to mount a primary campaign — their traditional associations were ill-equipped to do canvassing or precinct work — and they had no candidate. They created a series of ad hoc caucuses, like the Concerned Democrats, the Coalition for an Open Convention, the Coalition for a Democratic Alternative, and various other "dump Johnson" groups, to fill this vacuum, and then they persuaded Eugene McCarthy to run as their candidate against Johnson. Ultimately, both McCarthy and Robert Kennedy employed these jerry-built structures to help organize and sustain each other's primary campaign. When Robert Kennedy was murdered and Eugene McCarthy lost at the convention, the liberals decided not to dismantle the apparatuses they had built up, but to recast them into a single broad progressive coalition: the New Democratic Coalition (NDC).

At the time the notion of a magazine first entered my mind, I turned to the New Democratic Coalition for assistance. The NDC was a kibbutz of antiwar activists and political friends. Indeed, most of the young organizers of the McCarthy campaign and, later, of the 1969 Moratorium — persons like Sam Brown, David Mixner, and Harold Ickes, Jr. — were members. There were, too, for a time, a number of Kennedy followers involved, like Paul Schrade, the Western Division head of the United Auto Workers, who was one of the two original NDC national chairmen.

The organization was also an expanse of left-wing political ferment, comprising a network of liberal outposts, left over from the Johnson challenge of 1968, that crisscrossed the country. It extended into precincts and wards and reform clubs in at least twenty-five large states. The NDC was a group, I realized, from which *The New Democrat* might recruit correspondents from many states, and was a unique means by which our magazine could reach progressives throughout the country.

Since we also believed emphatically that, in order to reconstruct a liberal base in the party, it was necessary to go to the already organized liberal-left, the NDC was a natural ally. The NDC, by the nature of its membership and its crucial links to the Kennedy and McCarthy campaigns, was, along with the ADA (which served more as an idea source and congressional lobby for progressives than as a strictly political vehicle), the caucus par excellence for this sort of strategy.

So, in December 1969, Grier Raggio and I paid an informal visit to the Washington headquarters of the NDC, a small, bare office in Georgetown run by Don Greene, a young man once active in the McCarthy campaign. He greeted us affably, and we immediately launched into an impassioned request for help in getting *The New Democrat* off the ground. Greene sighed. It was clear that he had heard similar entreaties before. He lobbed a few incredulous queries in our direction about costs and funds. However, after much discussion, he agreed to give us some names for possible magazine correspondents, and he also agreed to exchange NDC mailing lists for free ads in our magazine on the condition that the NDC could retain a certain amount of the subscription take.

The arrangement was, like most things in left-wing politics, exceedingly loose and informal, infused with the saintly, unspoken trust that abounded throughout the movement. When we returned to New York, Michael Kramer, one of the young journalists who aided the magazine in its early days, culled the names of chapter heads from an NDC brochure and then persuaded a large number of them to become correspondents for the fledgling journal.

Most of the other attempts to effect exchanges with the NDC fell flat. When we tried to obtain the national NDC mailing lists, we discovered that there was no systematic catalogue of names except those in the possession of the state chapters; then we found that the local NDCs, in most cases, functioned with such irregularity that their rolls were not up-to-date. So we never obtained any NDC lists. We learned, too, that both the national and state offices printed newsletters only infrequently. Our magazine received one free advertisement in an amateurish NDC handout, which brought paltry results. The older liberal associations, like the ADA and the

NCEC, proved far more reliable than the NDC in exchanging lists.

The NDC, we soon divined, was more of an emotion in liberal minds than a corporeal institution. It was a coalition to honor the glorious legions of 1968, a meeting place for dissent within the party, a reference point for the left, a flag that sentimental liberals wanted to fly, but it was not like the AFL-CIO's COPE, a hard-nosed political operation that drew on limitless funds, ran an efficient headquarters, used computers, and lined its troops up professionally for its assaults on the citadels of the foe.

Even NDC's most cherished concept, that of becoming a coalition of minorities, labor, and white middle-class liberals, proved to be faulty from the beginning. The NDC's first national roster of officials included black leaders like the Reverend Channing Phillips of Washington and Julian Bond of Georgia, and Chicanos like Bert Corona of the Mexican-American Political Association. Donald Petersen, one of its two original leaders, a former McCarthy delegate from Wisconsin, set forth the NDC strategy in late 1968. "The old coalition that controlled the Democratic Party and elected its presidents from the time of FDR is no longer effective or appealing to the public. There have been too many social and demographic changes. We need in the party a new coalition that will include groups that have always been excluded — Negroes, Mexican-Americans, poor whites, and youth."[1]

We soon confronted a make-up of the NDC that was quite different from its theoretical one — that is, like every liberal coalition that preceded it, it was predominantly white, middle-class, and educated. The evidence, if one needed to see it, was on display at the NDC's first national convention, held in

Chicago in February 1970, which I covered for the magazine. The 500 delegates were overwhelmingly white, from academia and suburbia, and represented the bulk of McCarthy's constituency (though McCarthy did not attend). This comfortable class of Americans generated most of the political energy for the NDC. Not long afterward, indeed, most NDC leaders were willing to acknowledge, and even see merit in, their almost completely white roster. Bernard Sorokin, National Chairman of the NDC, told me, "We used to get upset, but no longer. Today every group — blacks, Puerto Ricans, women, Gays — is doing their own thing. We can still work with their organizations on issues and elections. We are what we are and the old hang-up is finished."[2]

The February convention was for me a revelation and a disappointment. It had a moment of bizarre bravado when the Chicago Seven defendants arrived to solicit funds for their defense from the assemblage. But the lack of minority people was painfully apparent. Only one black leader, George Wiley, head of the predominantly black National Welfare Rights Organization (NWRO), was present — to tongue-lash the NDC for its lack of commitment to his campaign for a $6500 guaranteed minimum income for a family of four. Also, months before the Chicago meeting, most of the Kennedy people had withdrawn from NDC; and, at the convention, Paul Schrade resigned his chairmanship, expressing his disappointment that the NDC had failed to organize the Democratic Party's most loyal voters — the blacks, the browns, and the blue-collars.[3] Marvin Madeson became the NDC's 1970 national chairman; he was a relatively unknown businessman from Missouri. Most of the delegates at Chicago seemed unclear about what the NDC should do next. Few seemed interested in the party reform struggles, and, curiously enough, many were hostile toward Senator George McGovern, whom they had formerly considered a blood-brother, because he had journeyed a few weeks before to Wyoming to speak on behalf of an NDC renegade, the hawkish Senator Gale McGee, for re-election.

This liberal backslide at Chicago led *The New Republic*'s usually sympathetic observer, Paul Wieck, to inquire, after the conference, "What Happened to the New Politics?" He sourly chided the NDC:

> If the politically adrift are looking to the New Democratic Coalition to seize control of the Democratic Party or launch a new party if necessary, they'd best forget it for the time being . . . If NDC is to become a potent national force in 1972, and it is anything but at the moment — it will have to cast a long shadow of powerful state and local organizations capable of electing large numbers of candidates.[4]

Wieck's perceptions were apt. Shortly after the convention, the national office, $20,000 in debt, shuttered its Washington headquarters. A token effort was made by Marvin Madeson to brace the national structure. Working out of his living room in St. Louis, Madeson plied his phone relentlessly, made unflagging sales pitches, dispatched a few newsletters, set up an internship program to train students to work on campaigns, and traveled to liberal conferences. It was to no avail; he failed to light a national prairie fire for the NDC.

However, there were some smaller NDC brush fires spreading in several states. We received a steady stream of reports on these little conflagrations, some ignited by caucuses loosely allied with the NDC, like the Concerned Democrats in Florida, the Massachusetts Political Action for Peace (Mass

PAX), the California Democratic Council, as well as some put ablaze by the national organization, like the New York state NDC. By May 1969, NDC existed in thirty-two states and had about 65,000 members, with ten other states showing some interest in setting up chapters.[5]

The common preoccupations of these state groups, as *The New Democrat*'s local correspondents reported, were frequent antiwar exercises against the Nixon administration — beginning with the 1969 Moratorium, followed by the petitions against the Cambodian invasion in 1970, and by fights for antiwar planks at state conventions. One new exercise that became fashionable was the movement for reforms. Missouri's activist chapter issued a nineteen-page blast at the regulars for noncompliance with the McGovern-Fraser guidelines. Other states regularly complained to the press. Yet the collective punch of all the antiwar and reform projects was, at best, a slap on the wrist of the administrations, state and federal.

The most publicized activity was the endorsement of local candidates. The involvement of the caucuses varied widely from state to state. Here also it might be added that, like Ring Lardner's ballplayer who wasn't a good fielder but also wasn't a good hitter, the NDC was not much good in local elections, either.

The caucus about which I was most knowledgeable was the New York state NDC, because *The New Democrat* offices were in the city. Many of my local political friends were, with varying degrees of good cheer, members. The NDC in New York state was the strongest of all the United States chapters, because, at its birth in 1969, it inherited a congeries of Democratic reform clubs, around 130, representing nearly 15,000 members. It was also the richest, because most of the wealthy liberals, who in the past had funded the antiwar movement and the earlier civil rights campaigns, lived in the city. The New York NDC's first endorsement in 1969 had turned out to be its luckiest — it backed John Lindsay, who became one of the few NDC-endorsed candidates to win office. The NDC blessed him for re-election on the Liberal line, shortly after he had lost the Republican primary. Once Lindsay gained office, though, he gave few city posts to workers from the NDC and soon forgot them. Many members later grew to resent his cavalier treatment and turned against him.

In 1970, the New York NDC, which by then numbered almost 25,000 members, held a convention to choose nominees for the statewide contests. The all-day session, held in a high-school auditorium in Manhattan, was a spirited affair. The turnout was impressive. The lobbying and the speeches and the demonstrations were serious and well organized and indicated that the candidates were earnest in their wooing of the NDC. Even *The New Republic* took notice, editorially extolling New York's NDC:

> We've heard for years that idealistic, issue-oriented Democrats are incapable of self-discipline that results in orderly procedures and a consensus behind qualified candidates. It's too bad these skeptics weren't at the New Democratic Coalition convention in New York City, February 28. Not only did nearly 400 delegates . . . dispense with politically inspired procedural flare-ups with a minimum of acrimony; they were able to deal with a wealth of talent available for major offices and come up with endorsements for all statewide offices by late afternoon.[6]

But this NDC convention never really resolved its basic dilemma — one that soon divided NDCs all over the nation — whether to work with the state Democratic parties and accept their nominees, or to act as a small left-wing party and insist on its own issues and candidates.[7] The New York NDC in 1970 muddled between the two extremes. It chose four candidates, all of whom fought primaries against party regulars. Two won — its nominees for attorney general and lieutenant governor. Then the NDC decided to back the remaining regulars along with its own survivors. All the designees lost in November.

By this time, many liberal political analysts were openly complaining about the NDC's lack of political realism. They charged the NDC with playing amateurish politics. For instance, all the people NDC favored for the November election were either Jewish or black — an affront to two other large ethnic blocs in New York state, the Irish and the Italians. Jack Newfield of *The Village Voice* said the initials "NDC" stood for "November Doesn't Count."

By 1973, the NDC's grace period among New York politicos had completely elapsed. During that year's mayoralty race, the NDC was castigated on all sides for its political obtuseness. First, the NDC endorsed Albert Blumenthal, a local state assemblyman, for mayor, over the favorite, Congressman Herman Badillo, a Puerto Rican — an act that enraged the large Puerto Rican constituency in the state. Then, after Blumenthal lost in the Democratic primary to Abe Beame, the man finally elected mayor, the NDC chose neutrality.

One faction thought the NDC should play by the rules of the game. Professor Dan Collins of the New York University Law School, the chairman of the New York NDC from 1969 to 1972, normally a soft-spoken and conciliatory man, scornfully reproached his old organization for "hypocrisy," in not supporting the primary winner selected by the majority of the

New York Democrats.[8] On the other hand, James Wechsler, the editor of the New York *Post*, wrote that the NDC's neutrality was a moral abdication of its endorsement of Al Blumenthal, who was still on the Liberal Party ticket in the November election. By staying on the sidelines, Wechsler asserted, the NDC had succumbed to the appeals for "party unity" and "political realism," which the old reformers like Herbert Lehman and Eleanor Roosevelt would have rejected out of hand.[9]

The difficulties of the New York NDC were very depressing insofar as they reflected the fate of liberalism in the seventies. It was clear that liberals needed to re-evaluate the NDC's role. On the one hand, they still required some sort of organization to fight in the Democratic Party for those controversial issues on the left that conventional politicians dodged. On the other hand, affiliated state NDCs (such as the New York NDC), were breaking apart over local endorsements. They could not pretend to be a party conscience when they got involved in local party brawls. Somehow, it was an untenable spot for NDC to be in: preaching reform but practicing old-style politics, and doing both ineffectually.

During the 1972 presidential primaries, however, the NDCs proved their value. Almost inadvertently, the NDCs — because they were the only progressive forums extant — became the crucial liberal brokers for the Democratic presidential race through special "rump" conventions in six critical primary states — five in the East (Maryland, Pennsylvania, Florida, New York, and Massachusetts) and one in the West (California). For the dispirited NDCs, the presidential contest was a tonic. It magnified and fortified and stimulated all their best qualities. The peculiar organizing talents of NDC members came to the fore in the din and bedlam of the presidential primary contests, as they had not in the unrewarding, fractious local races. In fact, the NDC's unusual preprimary convocations in 1972 miraculously transformed a weak and vulnerable candidate, George McGovern, into a genuine contender.

The six conventions, for the most part, were put together by leaders in those states where a sizeable liberal franchise already existed. The organizers were men and women still seared by the memories of Chicago in 1968, single-minded in their wish to have an impact on the nomination in 1972, and unwilling to be harassed by local party bosses. Thus state NDC leaders adopted the virtually unprecedented idea of using their own organizations to create ad hoc liberal conventions outside the party structure. The idea did have some vague precedents in the California Democratic Council, which, since the 1950s, had held statewide presidential caucuses, and in local ADA chapters, which in some states had served as gathering places for local liberals, where they could endorse candidates. But the NDC convocations were far more systematic and deliberate. They were patterned, in part, after the national conventions. They called for a large number of delegates, sometimes elected, sometimes just dues-paying members of NDC. They specifically aimed at influencing the primary outcome. They quite pointedly by-passed the state party machinery. They tried to guarantee a progressive presidential candidate political support within the state without having to make deals with local bosses. And finally, with the new reforms making practically all delegate positions contestable, the NDC conventions were designed to give the liberal candidate an extra boost with both money and volunteers.

In some cases, however, the ad hoc NDC conventions could also spell trouble for the candidate. For example, as Professor James MacGregor Burns has pointed out, the rules used by these gatherings were often inequitable. The participants were subject to poll taxes in the form of entry fees. There was little advance notice about the conventions. And the delegates were severely restricted by the "elite" who ran the meetings.[10] In a sense, while literally "open," the NDC assemblies were ideologically stacked. Furthermore, though the conventions provided useful publicity within the state for the candidate, they could, at the same time, inject the petty feuds of the coalition into the candidate's own headquarters. In some cases, NDC rivalries could actually hamper the ability of a presidential candidate to widen his appeal.

The McGovern strategists, although aware of the pitfalls, were desperately low in the polls and very conscious of the need to collect endorsements as quickly and as early as they could. They had always assumed that the route to the nomination, as a consequence of the reforms, was essentially via the left-wing, with the center playing a very small role. This, of course, accorded perfectly with the convictions of the NDCs. Rick Stearnes, the tactician responsible for guiding McGovern through the nonprimary states, asserted flatly that "the real basis of the McGovern campaign initially — until the point where the first primary successes scored — was the [Vietnam] war binding together and associating a faction in the party."[11] Gary Hart, the principal planner for McGovern's primary fights, regarded McGovern's main constituency as the people who made up the NDCs — "the Kennedy-McCarthy activists, the young, minority groups, antiwar organizations, women and others whose commitment to the principles of the Democratic Party generally outweighed the voice they had exerted in its affairs. This was a movement already in progress . . ."[12] Thus, the McGovern people hungrily sought out the NDC endorsements. And to the surprise of many, including myself, the role of the NDC was prophetic in the primaries.

The first rump caucus was held in mid-January in Massachusetts. McGovern's standing in the national Gallup poll was 3 percent. January, Hart later said, was "the Valley Forge of our campaign. We had almost no money — we were almost completely destitute. It was a very, very low period."[13] And *Newsweek*'s poll that month gave Massachusetts to Muskie with this comment: "With Kennedy out, power goes for Muskie; Lindsay a sleeper here." McGovern's name was never mentioned.[14]

Over 4000 people showed up on January 15, 1972, at Holy Cross College in Worcester. The participants included peace activists, Cambridge intellectuals, quarreling local factions, Nobel laureates, Kennedy followers and Kennedy haters, and an assortment of delegates committed to a variety of other causes. The caucus was sponsored by Mass PAX, a vigorous, liberal antiwar group whose leader, Jerome Grossman, served on the steering committee of the national NDC; and the Massachusetts Citizens for Participation in Politics (CPP), which had boosted Father Robert Drinan for his successful race for Congress in 1970. Both groups were associated with the national NDC. The Coalition of Black People and the National Youth Caucus also backed the convention.

Several of our magazine correspondents, including me, covered the convention. We had already angered Grossman by printing a piece on the convention's uncertain future.[15] However, the convention turned out to be well organized, even if an elaborate MIT computer system rigged up to count the ballots went, inevitably, awry. In a state with relatively few poor people, the caucus was primarily a suburban and middle-class fest. There were practically no regular politicians there; men like Congressman "Tip" O'Neill, or even Senator Edward Kennedy, would have seemed quite out of place. The auditorium seemed to glow with energy, with that passionate heat, or "intensity factor," which Joseph Rauh, Jr., once rated as the primary virtue of the emotional left-wing of the Democratic Party.

In three long, drawn-out ballots, the convention gave McGovern 62 percent of the vote, just over the 60 percent required for endorsement for the April 25 primary. Eugene McCarthy, the favorite of some caucus organizers, and the only candidate besides Representative Shirley Chisholm who attended, was too discredited and battered by his withdrawal from political life to raise more than 13 percent of the vote; and Muskie and Lindsay, with no apparent NDC support, boycotted the convention.

The result visibly buoyed up the McGovern campaign. Richard Dougherty, the press secretary, later wrote that the Massachusetts outcome "removed any lingering doubts about McGovern's having pre-empted virtually all the peace movement — once the exclusive turf of the poet-politician from Minnesota."[16] Our *New Democrat* correspondent observed that "the antiwar forces left Worcester with a renewed, if tenuous, sense of unity and purpose."[17]

Once again, we were taken aback by the lack of national press coverage. Most political writers who gave any notice at all to the convention ascribed little significance to McGovern's victory at Worcester. Many knowledgeable Democratic politicians supporting Muskie, Lindsay, or Humphrey downplayed the affair. The *New York Times* treated the event as a test of McGovern's campaign style — "radical in his ideas but entirely orthodox in his political approach" — and as a "harsh" defeat for McCarthy.[18]

What the outside observers did not perceive here were the nuances, the delicate shift in the winds, that Worcester represented. For the Massachusetts convention had infused new energy into the McGovern campaign — and this meant more volunteers, more money, more public acceptance. The signal to progressives around the country was that McGovern was the liberal's great hope. But no reporters picked up the message. The Mass Caucus later brought McGovern an overwhelming Massachusetts primary victory on April 25 — 51 percent of the vote and all of the state's delegates.

The following weekend, on January 22, McGovern also claimed the caucus of the Concerned Democrats of Florida, where the presidential primary was to take place on March 14. The assemblage gave McGovern 83 percent of its vote. As our correspondent, Edward Cohen, wrote after the endorsement, "If there is such a thing as a liberal establishment in Florida, it is firm in support of Senator George McGovern . . ."[19] That establishment, however, was quite modest, and was centered mainly in Miami. McGovern, anxious to save resources for the Wisconsin primary, spared only six paid staff members and $50,000 for the Florida primary. Gary Hart wrote that the McGovern forces "relied almost totally on the organization work of our state committee and local supporters."[20] McGovern survived the contest, in fact, on the backs of the Concerned Democrats, who beat the bushes for every liberal vote in the Dade County area — he also benefited, of course, from his surprise showing the week before in New Hampshire. McGovern received only 6 percent of the Florida vote, but this left him equal to John Lindsay, who had spent over $500,000 and had brought hundreds of campaign aides down from New York City for his effort. Since Mc-Govern had publicly underplayed his Florida involvement, it was Lindsay who was discredited by the small vote.

Also on the weekend of January 22, in Philadelphia, the Pennsylvania NDC's 1350 delegates gave McGovern 63 percent of their vote on the first ballot for its April 25 primary. Once again, as in the other states, this special meeting represented McGovern's only visible backing for the primary: a loose gathering of peace activists, reformers, Kennedy-McCarthy loyalists, and wealthy liberals. And McGovern, concentrating on a big turnout in Massachusetts and threatened by Humphrey's ties with labor, allocated practically no resources for the Pennsylvania primary. As Hart noted later, "Our base of support was essentially among the 1968 McCarthy supporters and antiwar elements. Although a number of these people were generous financially, it was not really enough to match the resources available to Humphrey."[21] Yet, with Muskie's dropout, McGovern polled 21 percent of the vote and he finished second to Humphrey in the delegate count — a modest victory, but essential to slowing Humphrey's drive.

The following weekend, on January 30, 1972, came Mc-Govern's most notable NDC triumph — the endorsement by the powerful liberal block in the country's second largest state after California, the New York state NDC. At this NDC convention, there was an aura of high expectation, encouraged by the strong antiwar emotions and bitter hatred of Richard

Nixon by the delegates. They regarded the NDC meeting as the moment when they would reassert control over their fate and select a progressive, who would finally win the presidency for them.

For McGovern, it was another dramatic coup. In a well-planned, well-oiled campaign, he picked up the normally fractious NDC legions of New York after three ballots, winning 69 percent of the vote. The winds were now blowing strongly in his direction. His victory obliterated the candidacy of John Lindsay by showing that the mayor had no progressive backing in his own backyard; and McCarthy's fading pretensions to the nomination were dashed when he received only 10 percent of the vote. The *New York Times* noted afterward that, while the "convention's endorsement is not binding, except morally, on the coalition's 128 clubs and 18,000 members throughout the state — it means substantial and organized support for Mr. McGovern in the June 20th primary . . ."[22] (McCarthy, with much the same backing, had won 87 of the state's 190 delegates in 1968). On June 20, McGovern, with the help of the local reform clubs, won 252 of the 276 delegates.

Professor Richard C. Wade of the City University of New York, the tactician who dictated McGovern's strategy at the convention, later agreed that "the NDC gave McGovern the endorsement of the left and knocked out all of our competitors — Lindsay, McCarthy, and Chisholm. This was crucial because in a close primary race you can't sacrifice even a small percentage of the progressive vote to another liberal. The NDC was critical in the primary contest." But Wade also had some doubts about the NDC's essential importance. "In the process of winning the NDC, we lost relationships with regulars in Westchester and Nassau County because the local

NDCs wouldn't deal at all with the professional politicians and wouldn't run joint delegate slates or combine organizational forces."[23]

The fifth endorsement came early in February, when McGovern plucked the Maryland NDC endorsement on the second ballot; and on May 16, with no investment of resources other than the NDC's volunteers, he came in third in the state primary with 22 percent of the vote, closely behind Humphrey — while Wallace won with 39 percent. McGovern was second to Wallace in delegates. The small coterie of antiwar activists and reformers who coalesced in the NDC in this generally conservative state salvaged the McGovern operation just as McGovern was hitting his stride against Humphrey nationally.

McGovern's only tumble came in March in California, when the California Democratic Council (CDC) declined to endorse him. The CDC was one of the earliest precursors of the state NDCs, a liberal coalition that had influenced state politics since 1953, when it was formed in the wake of Stevenson's presidential loss. Though in 1972 it was just regaining status in the state after cracking apart under the emotions of the war, still McGovern could obtain only 56 percent of the 60 percent required for official CDC support. Nonetheless, many of the 150 clubs throughout the state and many of their 12,000 members organized for McGovern in the primary. And despite a rough contest with Humphrey, McGovern, with momentum, plentiful contributions, and a winning scent about him, outpolled his rival on June 6 and won all 271 delegates there under the controversial winner-take-all rule.

For the media, though, McGovern's pursuit of the NDC was, all along, a nonevent. A close examination of newspapers like the *New York Times* and the Washington *Post,* and even progressive journals like *The New Republic* revealed little or no attention given to the NDC conventions. From the reports of our correspondents, though, we gained a different impression of NDC's importance. It seemed apparent that, in the first three months of 1972, the public endorsements by NDC-type caucuses in five states resurrected the McGovern campaign just before the crucial New Hampshire primary, when it was tottering on its last legs, penniless and friendless. The endorsements suddenly made credible McGovern's claim to grass-roots strength in the large industrial states. The 60 percent rule in force at the first five caucuses indicated that there was a substantial array of people behind McGovern. The NDC espousals helped to eliminate the competing claims of liberals, like McCarthy, Lindsay, Chisholm, any of whom might have destroyed McGovern's campaign. Most of all, the fact that the endorsements occurred in concert gave McGovern momentum, something he could not have acquired had the caucuses not existed. Though national press coverage of these meetings was sorely limited, the NDC beacons were flashing to the politicians that McGovern was the progressives' choice.

Our relationship with the NDC during this period was mutually supportive. *The New Democrat* and the NDC were agreed on all issues. We drew our ideas, our writers, our subscribers from the same well. We made a special effort to print notes on NDC activities as well as to give continuous coverage to NDC conventions, believing that the NDC filled a singular niche in Democratic Party affairs that no other organization, including the ADA, could fill. During this period, we even worked out an arrangement for a regular NDC column in *The*

New Democrat through Linda Davidoff, a bright, resourceful young woman who was a vice-chairwoman of the New York NDC and the secretary of the national NDC. However, the person she persuaded to write the column produced one contribution and then disappeared. Ms. Davidoff herself in the end was perhaps our best source of information on matters inside the NDC.

When I joined the McGovern campaign, however, my relationship with the NDC cooled. It was an object lesson in how institutions shape friendships. In mid-June, early on in my job on McGovern's platform staff, Ted Van Dyk, McGovern's issues director, asked me and Verne Newton, the magazine's investigative reporter, who had also joined the McGovern staff, to go as McGovern's representatives to a meeting in New York City, which the NDC had requested for the purpose of discussing the upcoming platform hearings. Van Dyk was uncertain about the nature of NDC's motivations but he wanted us to be there to "stroke" the officers of the coalition.

Linda Davidoff, our NDC contact, and Bernard Sorokin, the latest national chairman, a dentist from Hartford, Connecticut, were among the NDC members present at the conference. Much to my chagrin, I found all NDC eyes resting on me somewhat like those of stern doctors examining a patient for signs of disease. Shifting uneasily, I listened as Sorokin launched into a disquisition about the NDC's platform — a lengthy thirty-three-page document that the coalition had gathered from some ninety-one witnesses, including former Senator Eugene McCarthy, Gloria Steinem, David Dellinger, Marcus Raskin, Senators Fred Harris, Edmund Muskie, and our own leader, George McGovern. At the conclusion, Sorokin explained that the NDC was very concerned about whether there was some way the McGovern staff could insure that the NDC's ideas would be considered and perhaps incorporated into the drafting of the Democratic platform.

None of us McGovern folk had instructions from Van Dyk on how to reply to the NDC's requests. After hemming and hawing a bit, we collectively hedged. Linda Davidoff glared at me. Sorokin and the others were somewhat irritated. I felt a little ashamed because I did not seem to be standing up for the NDC, but I was not exactly in a position to impale McGovern on my special lance. My uneasiness intensified. Finally, we agreed to have a second meeting just before the platform hearings to see if McGovern's positions could be accommodated to those of the NDC and vice versa, though, in truth, I realized the candidate's were not too different from the organization's. Later, I noted in a memorandum to Ted Van Dyk that I thought the NDC, in its evident coolness, was only playing the role to which it had assigned itself — that of the left-wing watchdog. The NDC people, I wrote, are not really "disillusioned with McGovern; they're just trying to represent their interests. They are all practical men and women . . . (but) they have an obligation to their own constituencies, which they must fulfill, even if it means sending out many minority planks to the convention floor." I might have added that, in their minds, I seemed to be another antagonist they now had to deal with.

At the second meeting, held in mid-June, Ted Van Dyk was present and delivered the McGovern exposition on the platform issues. Basically, he told the NDC that he was perfectly happy if it went ahead and lobbied with the platform delegates for its proposals. The McGovern people would not, he said, interfere with the NDC, nor would they assist it. The McGovern delegates would simply report out the platform that McGovern wanted without a lot of controversial issues tacked to it — like abortion. I think the NDC picked up the meaning of Van Dyk's quietly spoken caveat.

Van Dyk told me later that some of the people at the meeting were hunting for jobs in the campaign. I realized that that off-hand observation just about summed up the attitude of most McGovern people toward the NDC. Since there was no real issue cleavage between the coalition and the candidate, except over abortion and some tax matters, since the NDCs had actively endorsed McGovern in five states and in many nonprimary states, and since many NDC people were already involved in the McGovern campaign, it was difficult for wiser heads at the headquarters to understand how the NDC could or should be further accommodated. The NDC's frequent meetings were seen thus as a bid by a few NDC officials for influence in the future McGovern administration.

The NDC representatives, nevertheless, felt upset at the McGovern staff's aloofness, rightfully or not. I think they came to see, perhaps like many of the other new movement groups in the campaign, that once the McGovern campaign had received their backing, it was less responsive to them, not out of indifference — it was a crusade of authentic liberal commitment — but because it was quickly absorbed by other priorities. The NDC, however, did not like to be neglected now that it was so near to real power — despite the fact that at the next critical juncture, the Miami convention, which it wished to influence, it was in a powerful position; most delegations included a handful of coalition members and the New York delegation was one-third NDC.

In Miami, though, the NDC demanded another meeting with the McGovern staff. Van Dyk once again threw Verne Newton and me into the lion's den. We went to a small room in McGovern's headquarters hotel. The atmosphere was chilly, and it was not just the air conditioning. A few people grumbled that McGovern was selling them out on abortion, radical tax planks, and some other issues. I knew there was nothing substantive I could say, so I reassured them that Mc-Govern had not changed his basic positions — and then I quickly departed.

I did not spy the NDC again after that meeting. It simply vanished from sight. Its leaders dispersed to their several states, and its political visibility rapidly shrank. We received no more complaints from the NDC over neglect. The reason for this abrupt disappearance was not because the NDC people were deserting McGovern. On the contrary, I frequently encountered local chapter heads of the NDC, all working feverishly to bail out the Democratic ship. Rather, the NDC's influence as an organization diminished in the fall race because it was essentially a creature of the primary stage. That was when its small, tenacious band of activists, working within the limited confines of the sparse Democratic primary turnouts, could organize precinct by precinct for the election of McGovern delegates and make a perceptible impact.

After the election, I found a lot of liberal politicians shaking their heads at the NDCs and beginning to wonder whether the essential role of the coalitions should not be re-evaluated or, more drastically, ended. The nature of the doubts puzzled me, because I was convinced that the NDCs had actually given McGovern a crucial psychological lift during an early and desperate stage in his candidacy, and thereafter had be-

131

come substantially inoperative, without means of doing harm. It did not seem correct to finger the NDCs as the left-wing ghouls who alone had besmirched McGovern as a "radical." Some shrewd liberal tacticians, however, argued quite persuasively that after McGovern's nomination the NDC endorsements constituted an albatross around his neck. Other equally passionate activists contended exactly the reverse — that without the NDC's initial support McGovern would never have won the nomination at all.

In New York state, the man who ran the McGovern campaign, Richard C. Wade, asserted unequivocally to me that

the price NDC exacts is so high on a candidate that it soon exceeds the cost. For instance, we spent an inordinate amount of time on fulfilling the compliance requirements for our candidate at some eighty NDC clubs in the pre-endorsement stage. We had to send speakers to the clubs around the clock. We could have spent all this time much more fruitfully and profitably in organizing the state for McGovern through local liberal groups. In addition, the executive committee was a continuing problem. No one can sit on it who has won an election. This means that no successful politician can be on the committee, though those who lose can serve. So the people who really controlled the NDC tended to be liberal professionals. Furthermore, the board was closed — not in the upper-class sense of elitism but in the cronyism sense — where everybody knows everyone else. The people on it were more interested in perpetuating NDC's institutional existence than in winning elections.

Today these people still hold power in the NDC. But they do not seem to notice what is wrong. They do not seem agitated over the fact that NDC is attracting no new members — except those brought in for endorsement's sake, that its average age is older every year, that its base is shrinking. The city reform clubs will ultimately disaffiliate from the NDC because the incessant factionalism has become too much of a burden. Someday a liberal Democrat will surely win a primary by running against the NDC. In nineteen seventy-six, no liberal presidential candidate can afford to care whether he gets the NDC endorsement or not. NDC's future, I guess, lies only in the suburbs where no Democratic organization exists. Once the NDC dies, there will always be another liberal coalition to replace it. This is because all the liberals know one another and will want to make a fresh start on some other issue. Liberal groups are as permanent as the regular organizations. I only hope, however, that the replacement is a coalition that does not exclude successful liberal politicians.[24]

This dire view, I found, was common among liberal activists who had occasion to deal with the NDC and were exasperated, hurt, or angered by the treatment the NDC handed out to them. Even the New York NDC's former chairman, Dan Collins, told me "there were times when I thought I was in crazyland . . . NDC people are zealots and they will not forgive errors."[25]

Nonetheless, the New York NDC, despite its series of statewide defeats and despite the liberal bitterness, still survives tenaciously in New York state in the mid-seventies. This is a tribute of some backhanded sort to the potency of the NDC elixir among a certain segment of white, middle-class, emotional liberals in New York and in many other states. Indeed, a number of the local NDC leaders I talked with expressed the notion that the NDC holds a unique place in American politics. Arnold Weiss, Dan Collins' successor as the New York NDC chairman, who works as a lawyer on Wall Street, spoke rather dispassionately about NDC's future:

There is no reason for the NDC to die. We are over twenty-five percent of the state Democratic Committee's membership. We are cutting the edge for the new issues in the party — sexism, racism, the unequal distribution of wealth. Our approach, which some people criticize as elitist, has hurt some Democratic candidates in the short run, but we are in it for the long run to help the groups oppressed by the political system — and in the long run we aid them by our militancy. Frankly, somebody has to start to raise issues on the left. We play that role. I guess it would be much easier to elect more people if we stayed away from issues, but there would be no point to the NDC if we did.[26]

Linda Davidoff, a friend again after the election, also explained to me: "People accuse us of being purist. But we have a job to do. We have to play a role of representing the left. So we get abrasive. But we are not unrealistic. We do compromise sometimes. We do understand that in order for a Democratic candidate to win the individual may have to move to the center."[27]

My own opinion of the NDC is closer to Weiss's than to Wade's. The NDC, it seems to me, is not likely to die soon. It is too firmly rooted in liberal ideological soil; there is always a constituency of white, middle-class activists looking for a political role. The NDC might shrink in size; it might join forces with another progressive organization (at one point, the NDC approached the ADA about merging but with no results); it might be riven and battered by internal conflict. But its passionate, committed troops form a durable regiment in the army of American reformers.

Still, the NDCs remain fragile precisely because they depend so much on emotions aroused by candidates or issues. For example, in 1974, in the most liberal of all the states in the union, Massachusetts, the local version of the NDC, CPPAX (Citizens for Participation in Political Action), was not able to bestir many of its members to run for delegates to the Democratic Party's midterm convention. CPPAX and its allies had controlled the entire state delegation in 1972 for McGovern. Why this drop-off? Partly because the Massachusetts regulars reasserted themselves, and partly because, as Jerome Grossman, one of the founders of the progressive caucus, said, ". . . our people are issue oriented and they are hard to turn on if there are no issues."[28]

Yet the NDCs go on. Having survived a truncated presidential contest in 1968 and a full-blown one in 1972, having passed through financial crises in every year of their existence, NDCs have acquired a certain resilience. They are factors in at least seventeen states. NDC chapters have some 30,000 affiliated members; in 1974, many elected delegates to the midterm Democratic conference, notwithstanding Massachusetts' dismal showing. The NDCs intend to play a significant role again in the 1976 Democratic primaries. Any person who wishes to get some sense of the left-of-center thinking in this country will still turn to the NDCs for illumination.

Even as a national organization, the NDC continues to appear at every political meeting it can take part in (especially the Democratic National Committee), though it is still not listened to very seriously in discussions about issues. Only the ADA, the most powerful of the established reform groups, with a strong, centralized national office in Washington and a well-organized dues structure, is able to publicize the issues that truly sway liberals.

Yet the NDCs are, as Representative Bella Abzug once remarked, an ethnic bloc — of white, middle-class, educated liberals. And that is a bloc that many candidates who seek reform support must court in a number of the large Northern and Eastern industrial states if they wish to get money and volunteers. So, while it is clearly possible to by-pass the NDC, it is difficult to disregard it. That is where its continuing power lies.

☆

The Reformers Rally
in the House

THE IDEOLOGICAL LEFT in the House of Representatives has always foundered for lack of organization. In the early fifties, it was a scattered handful of backbenchers crying fitfully in a conservative wilderness. In the late fifties, the left formed a loose alliance of liberal congressmen, the Democratic Study Group (DSG), to raise a banner in Congress. In the sixties, when the Senate came under the domination of the liberals, the House progressives still languished. Finally, in the seventies, the liberals transformed their study group into a sophisticated political operation and revitalized progressive power in the House.

When I first visited Washington with *The New Democrat* still unborn, friends urged me to go see the DSG for writers, ideas, and information about progressive politics on the Hill. The DSG in late 1969 was poised to break out of its isolation in the House. The members had just refashioned the staff, bringing in a quiet-spoken, brilliant former newspaperman, Richard Conlon, as the executive director. Conlon had, himself, hired a bright, young supporting group of researchers, led by Rick Merrill, a red-headed, knowledgeable young man in his early thirties, cut in the antiestablishment mold of the sixties' generation.

I approached the DSG gingerly. I was still somewhat disbelieving, after the House's long-standing and vocal hawkishness on the war, that any progressive bloc could possibly prosper in Congress. However, wanting some connection with liberals on the Hill in order to flesh out the political coverage of the magazine, I set up an appointment early in December 1969 to confer with Rick Merrill. Then, on a wintry day, I trudged into the rather shabby, darkened offices of the DSG, hidden away on one of those interminable corridors in the Mussolini complex of buildings that house all the congressional offices. I met Merrill in a DSG anteroom whose walls were plastered with antiwar signs, peace emblems, and Moratorium banners. Merrill politely led me into his small chamber in the back. I sat down and then described the projected magazine and our desire for a possible tie-in with liberals in Congress.

Merrill was enthusiastic. He readily offered to send DSG publications to *The New Democrat* free of charge once we got started. (Under Conlon's tutelage the DSG was now mailing out a blizzard of legislative memos, weekly staff bulletins and digests on upcoming liberal issues, vote books, and special fact sheets on major bills listing their pros and cons for liberals.) He also suggested that *The New Democrat* and the DSG might be able to exchange mailing lists sometime — though we later never collected enough money to pay the postage or the stationery costs. In addition, he mentioned the names of young people working on the Hill who might serve as Washington correspondents for the journal. Merrill gave me one name in particular, that of Mike Duberstein, a legislative aide to Congressman Ronald Dellums of California, probably the most radical representative in the House.

The Reformers Rally in the House

Duberstein was a freaky character — he reminded some of his friends of Serpico, the idiosyncratic cop who blew the whistle on New York City police corruption. He had a walrus mustache, a hip lifestyle, and an offbeat view of Congress. When I got in touch with him, Duberstein signed on to write a regular column for *The New Democrat* called "The Congressional Watch." His first piece came out in our inaugural issue in April 1970, and thereafter he was the most prolific contributor to the magazine until the very last issue. He wrote most pieces under his pseudonym, "W. I. Zard," because he did not want to embarrass his employer.

Duberstein's opening salvo, "A BAS Seniority," succinctly spelled out the central issue that DSG progressives faced at the beginning of the new decade. Quoting from the DSG's own lengthy study of seniority, Duberstein noted that:

(1) one of three Democratic committee and subcommittee chairmen vote against party programs and against the majority of their colleagues more frequently than does the average Republican chairman (2) seniority gives undue power to a region — the South — which votes overwhelmingly against Democratic presidential candidates (3) there's been a steady increase in the average ages of committee chairmen. Only three are now under 60, 8 are in their 60's, 7 are in their 70's, and 3 in their 80's (4) the average chairman can expect to hold power for at least a full decade and frequently longer (5) at the same time, though, Congress itself is younger, less tied to the past. Nearly 60% of the current House were elected since 1961.[1]

In short, this meant that those who held power as a result of being part of the Democratic majority were, in fact, using that power to undercut the policies favored by the Democratic majority. The DSG report, Duberstein concluded hopefully, might put some heat on Congress "to bring about meaningful changes in the most conservative of all public institutions," and particularly now, he said, because the DSG and its moderate allies were acting more and more effectively as a "Shadow Congress." But he warned that "not even the wildest dreamers see total victory within the near future."[2]

Notwithstanding Duberstein's journalistic caution, the DSG was on the move. The staff, which I continued to see while on information-gathering trips to Washington, were excited by the DSG's venture into the never-never land of structural reform, one of those perennial challenges that, in the past, the DSG had acknowledged but had somehow never confronted. The 140-odd members of the DSG, and the DSG's smaller executive committee, were now meeting regularly at private sessions to plot out strategy. They were concentrating on specific rules changes — lifting the secrecy in House floor and committee votes, electing committee chairmen, and distributing power more equitably in the House.

It was a rather dramatic step up for the DSG. For years, the overwhelming majority of representatives had been conservative and regarded the DSG as some sort of rallying point for "radicals." The idea of a progressive caucus had seemed improbable when it was first advanced in the House in 1956 by Congressman Eugene McCarthy, but after the 1958 elections resulted in a massive influx of liberals, a formal structure began to evolve. The DSG hired an executive director and began to work out tactics to sneak or leapfrog liberal legislation past the conservatives who ruled the House committees. In the 1960s, the DSG's intensive labors bore only occasional fruit, though its membership gradually climbed to over 100 members. It helped make some moderately progressive changes in the House Rules Committee in 1961; it stripped seniority from two conservative Southern Democrats who supported Goldwater in 1964; in 1965 it forced the passage of a rule that automatically brought legislation to the floor if the Rules Committee did not act within twenty-one days. But it generally took outside direction on domestic and foreign programs — from two Democratic presidents, Kennedy and Johnson; and it divided over the Vietnam War.

Then, in 1969, according to the bearded, gravel-voiced Richard Conlon, the DSG changed. The election of Richard Nixon frightened even the most moderate Democrats. At that time, Conlon reminisced,

> we were vitally concerned that some sort of energetic liberal opposition had to be developed to head off Nixon from dismantling all of the Great Society programs and prolonging the war. The Democratic leadership was faltering, and conservatives controlled most of the committees. The liberals, labor Democrats, progressive moderates, and big-city regulars had a clear majority in the Democratic caucus, but never got any power. How to change this? We began to look for any loose brick — any weak fixture — in the walls of the House. Congressman James O'Hara [of Michigan], then Chairman of the DSG, asked for ideas. Most progressives were totally confused about power relationships in the House. All of a sudden it became clear to O'Hara that the members had to learn about the rules' complexities of the House if they wanted to change it. This meant a long-term educational effort by the DSG to make progressives conscious of the reforms that were really needed. This led to the idea of a monthly caucus.[3]

Up until 1969, the caucus had been the private preserve of the Speaker. It met one day every two years at the start of each new Congress to elect the Democratic leadership. Rayburn and McCormack had never permitted the caucus to be employed for any actions independent of their control, so debates on other issues were always perfunctory. Members had the power to convene the caucus for special purposes, but were too fearful of offending the Speaker to do so. As long as the caucus was only an occasional phenomenon, many militant progressives regarded it with contempt. They were not convinced that they could take control of party policy and decision-making through monthly meetings.

Inspired by O'Hara's suggestion, however, the DSG plotters began to discuss with Speaker McCormack the idea of a monthly caucus. After assessing the strength of the newly activated DSG, McCormack capitulated. The DSG now had a means of acting upon the House to press the Democratic leadership on controversial issues. As the wily O'Hara later explained to me, "Once we had the beast to ride every month, not every two years, we knew we could transform the House."[4]

But, Conlon pointed out, "the most significant change of all of them was the next one — the teller vote reform which we passed a year later, in nineteen seventy. Decades from now it will be seen as the single most important measure to increase public accountability of congressmen — and to make votes on legislation more fairly reflect progressive strength in the House."[5]

There is no easy way to describe how the teller vote distorted voting patterns in the House. It is enough to say that it arose in the past as a concession to efficiency, and led the House to operate on two sets of rules when considering amendments to bills. The first set was the formal procedure applicable to regular sessions, where debate was regulated, votes were recorded, and the quorum was a majority of the House — that is, 218 members. Then a second set of rules permitted a smaller quorum of 100 members and outlawed roll-call votes on amendments; instead, votes were by voice or by division (everybody standing in place) or by teller (members filing by two men who count their yeas and nays). These rules came into play when the House suspended its regular rules and became the Committee of the Whole. Here no vote was recorded.

The conservatives had historically used the Committee of the Whole to great advantage. Committee chairmen could, for several reasons, usually depend on liberals not to be on the floor when liberal amendments were up for consideration. First, there was a customary deference to the chairmen on amendments, even among progressives. This often led some liberals to issue public statements in support of a bill and then privately vote against the legislation in order to placate their chairmen and obtain occasional favors. Then, there was no disciplinary system to keep liberals on the floor. Liberals, observed Conlon, "are activists. They either are working hard for their constituents because many come from marginal districts or they are out attending meetings to save the world." So even a DSG whip system failed to round up liberals. Only conservatives, most of them from safe districts, could afford to stay on the floor for hours through unimportant debate. Finally, the nonrecorded vote enabled many congressmen to take a walk on a controversial issue. Indeed, less than one-third of the House participated in nonrecorded votes, which were often the most important. To pass the teller reform, then DSG chairman Don Fraser of Minnesota reached out to liberal Republicans for help. He got sympathizers in the opposition to agree on a reform that would empower twenty members to call for a recorded vote on an amendment even if it had already been voted on by voice or division vote. Next, he persuaded Majority Whip "Tip" O'Neill, himself a member of the DSG, to sponsor the measure, thereby converting many Democratic regulars to the change. The DSG also had a few happy publicity coups, including some excellent "anti-secrecy" editorials in newspapers around the country stimulated by a massive letter-writing campaign directed by the DSG. The change passed toward the end of 1970.

The differences in the House were dramatic. Members poured back onto the floor because they could not afford to look like absentees, and conservatives were more accountable to the changing sentiments of their constituents. Congressman O'Hara remarked to me with some irony: "It is a marvelous sight to behold three hundred and fifty or more men and women on the floor for most votes."[6] A DSG report issued one year later described in detail the massive alteration in voting habits. Whereas in 1970 liberals seldom won a single amendment on the nonrecorded vote, in 1971 the liberals won one-fourth of the newly recorded votes, and the conservatives, who had been accustomed to winning them all, took only one-half. (The rest of the votes involved minor housekeeping issues.[7]) The DSG tasted its first substantial victory under the new system when, in March of 1971 — just six months after the reform had taken effect — the House defeated the supersonic transport plane (SST) on a recorded vote, 217–204 — the same bill that, in 1970, had passed on a nonrecorded vote, 102–86.

At *The New Democrat*, we were preoccupied with national party reform. Had it not been for Duberstein's articles, we should have been unaware of the fundamental changes in the House. Most national reporters did not fully understand House politics and therefore did not give prominent coverage to the structural reforms. However, Duberstein's pieces made clear the fact that a reform within a reform was going on in the Democratic Party (and, by extension, in the Republican Party, since some of its members also backed the teller vote reform), and that these basic changes were just as important in enlarging liberal power as were the national party reforms. Paradoxically, these changes were occurring just when Richard Nixon was going around the country talking about the "silent majority" and its conservative hold on Congress.

However, as Mike Duberstein reported, following the teller vote, DSG progress was painfully slow. Shortly after the enactment of the change, the Democratic caucus passed only one more package of reforms, in 1971. These included a number of recommendations produced by a Democratic committee originally set up by the caucus at the DSG's insistence and chaired by Representative Julia Butler Hansen (Washington). These reforms limited members to one subcommittee chairmanship each and established a procedure by which ten members could call for a secret vote on chairmen. Though the subcommittee limitation did substantially shorten the period a new congressman had to wait for a chairmanship by opening up nineteen new slots, and though challenges to entrenched chairmen were now possible, neither reform really shook up the seniority process.

The Hansen recommendations, as Duberstein wrote later, unlike the teller change, were essentially "minor alterations in the seniority system." Any basic changes the liberals espoused

> lost right down the line. The congressional establishment reaffirmed its strong Nineteenth Century setting. Of course, liberals lost because they thought that the establishment would respond to the rising demands by the public that their representatives put the public interest ahead of their own ego trips —

145

as well as feeling that some response would be forthcoming to countermand the image of Congress' hopeless ineptness in performing its own functions. Instead — with few exceptions — the response was utterly reactionary . . . House liberals could have coalesced and massed for change. But they didn't . . . Once again liberals were disorganized and over-petty. Once again strategy was confused with manipulations.[8]

A few months later, in the spring of 1971, exasperated by the lack of dynamism in the House, Duberstein wrote sadly: "In many ways, the House can be viewed within a cybernetic framework. Years must pass before the House leadership — read that the center-right of the party — finally realizes that problems exist (i.e., that issues are more than abstractions) and at the same time generates momentum to deal with them. Usually once the intervening period has passed, the nature of the initial problem has changed significantly. The result is legislation geared to yesterday's conditions."[9]

For the next two years, the DSG's reform movement marked time. Although the group was pleased with the monthly caucus and the teller vote reform, it turned inward for a number of reasons: it was momentarily exhausted by its exertions in 1969 and 1970, but mainly it wished to focus more actively on the drawn-out, searing issue of the war.

First, however, the chairman in 1971–73, Phillip Burton of California, wanted to entice more moderates and centrists into the DSG in order to broaden its influence. This was a useful and neglected activity, and the DSG did grow in size through Burton's frenetic proselytizing. Burton, a hulking, talkative, driven reformer, described a determined strategy for rejuvenating the liberals:

By and large we had the smell of losers when I took over the DSG in March nineteen seventy-one. The feeling in the House

146

was that we were nice, hard-working guys with no political sense. I personally felt the study group was a small clique of self-serving, posturing liberals working in a very elitist manner without being in touch with the political currents in the Congress. I licked the loser image by making the DSG completely self-supporting through increasing dues and recruiting more members — from ninety-two when I came in to one hundred and sixty-five when I left. Also we began to behave like a majority — after all we had the most votes in any caucus meeting — so the Democratic leadership listened seriously to us.[10]

During Burton's tenure, the DSG continued in a low-key way to concentrate on House reforms. Burton directed his energies into a stint as the DSG representative on the second Hansen Reform Committee, the caucus committee that quietly worked on further structural changes — spurring a second big round of reforms in 1973. He was the DSG watchdog but, some of his critics allege, his service on the Hansen Committee allowed the study group's own reform commitment to lag. Mike Duberstein was particularly caustic; month after month, in his "Congressional Watch," he bemoaned the decline of the DSG, and raised anew the question of whether progressives would ever really shatter the conservative domination in the House.

But for Duberstein — and most reformers — perhaps the most profound DSG disappointment came over the issue of Vietnam. The inability to push for antiwar legislation for so many years — partly because of a split within DSG ranks that lasted until 1970 — was a bitter reflection on the DSG's actual weakness in the House. If the reformers — who, with labor Democrats, progressive moderates, and big-city regulars, were now a majority of the Democratic Caucus — had been able to organize to surmount the procedural obstacles, they might

147

have brought antiwar measures to the floor and at least demonstrated growing congressional opposition to the Vietnam policy. But their incapacity to change procedures was a canker sore eating away at their spirit in the late sixties and early seventies. If anything made DSG members in the House determined to reform their body, it was the obscenity of the continuing war.

Duberstein's distraught pieces placed the brunt of the blame squarely on the cautious House leadership. He devoted columns to the Speaker's or his lieutenants' apathy over Vietnam. In April 1971, Duberstein reported, progressives tried to get a vote on antiwar legislation, but the Democratic leadership postponed the caucus; Duberstein attacked the House stewards as "troglodytes when it comes to foreign policy." In June of that year, Congressman Dellums held an ad hoc hearing on American war crimes in Southeast Asia. Duberstein noted that Speaker Albert, under pressure from right-wingers, tried to deny Dellums room space for the inquiry. In mid-October, Albert and Majority Leader Hale Boggs sabotaged a House vote on the Mansfield amendment, which would have withdrawn all United States forces from Indochina in six months subject to the release of all POWs, even though, as Duberstein wrote, "well over half of the Democrats in the House had gone on record for complete withdrawal . . ." In March 1972, Duberstein said resignedly of the House: "the status-quo is the way of life, the benchmark. It represents the ability to get re-elected." Only in the summer of 1972, in the last issue of *The New Democrat*, did Duberstein begin to detect the possibility of change. By then, the Democratic Caucus at DSG insistence had passed a resolution sponsored by House Democratic Whip O'Neill to instruct Democratic members of the House Foreign Affairs

Committee to vote out an antiwar measure — the first time the caucus had ordered any committee to take such a policy action. This step represented, Duberstein asserted, "the strongest action taken within the Caucus and [is] an indication that the Caucus may develop into a forum for real debate rather than a sham meeting-ground."[11] Unfortunately, nothing came out of the Foreign Affairs Committee because of its Dixiecrat majority.

Six months after Duberstein's final lament, the DSG finally saw a new opportunity for action. It began to use the caucus to initiate a new round of serious proposals against the war. In February 1973, the DSG prevailed upon the Democrats to establish a new policy organ called the Democratic Steering and Policy Committee, chaired by the Speaker and composed of twenty-three Democrats, all generally progressive. The committee was authorized to recommend new Democratic policies to the House. But its main purpose was to place both the progressive majority in the party — a majority reflected in the composition of the Steering Committee — and the party leadership over the heads of the recalcitrant conservatives who chaired the crucial committees on issues of major importance to the Democratic Party, particularly Indochina.

The DSG Steering Committee maneuver passed through the caucus because the DSG obtained the backing of O'Neill and Albert, both of whom felt the committee would strengthen their collective powers as House leaders. And, though the DSG did not bruit it about, the passage of the reform also marked the final major step forward in the DSG's effort to bring about policy changes. The Steering Committee was the last building block the DSG needed to construct an unbeatable majority against the war.

With its reforms, the DSG took the offensive brilliantly

against Nixon's Indochina policies in the first month of 1973. First, the DSG exploited the outrage that most Democrats felt in December 1972 over the Christmas bombing of Hanoi. At the January caucus of the new year, DSG members introduced a resolution placing the Democratic Party in the House on record for the first time against further United States involvement in Indochina. They did this by threatening to stall Albert's re-election as Speaker unless he abandoned his resistance to an antiwar resolution. Albert reluctantly gave in and the motion passed, 154–75. Then the DSG made a public row over a Department of Defense request to transfer funds for financing further aerial bombardment in Cambodia. The study group leaders alerted the Steering Committee, which, on the basis of the caucus' January antiwar stand, voted 18 to 3 against the transfer, and directed the next party caucus to reject the proposals of the Department of Defense. The Steering Committee's action by-passed the conservative House Appropriations Committee, which had jurisdiction over the legislation and had already killed a similar proposal. Finally, the DSG went back to the caucus with the Steering Committee resolution and won a 144 to 22 vote in favor of canceling the funds transfer and stopping the B-52 raids. In May 1973, the measure finally went to the floor at a time when the Gallup polls showed overwhelming public opposition to the bombing. The vote to stop the transfer was recorded for public scrutiny by the House tellers. It passed, 219–188.

Speaker Albert, Majority Leader O'Neill, and three out of the four deputy whips supported the antitransfer position, a signal change from the year before when both Albert and his then Majority Leader, Hale Boggs, had backed Nixon over war legislation. Thirteen of twenty Democratic chairmen also voted for the stance, including many who turned against the war for the first time like Chet Holifield (California) of Government Operations, Wright Patman (Texas) of Banking and Currency, and Melvin Price (Illinois) of the Ethics Committee. Other senior Democrats switched their votes: John Rarick (Louisiana), William Randall (Missouri), James Delaney (New York), John Murphy (New York), Clement Zablocki (Wisconsin), Jack Brooks (Texas), and, significantly, Richard Bolling (Missouri), a maverick reformer from past DSG days who for years had supported the war.

And the votes were no aberration. In June 1973, the House voted in a 204 to 204 tie for an even tougher antibombing resolution barring the administration from using any "heretofore appropriated" funds for Cambodian air warfare. Ultimately, the House and Senate struck a compromise with the President, and on August 15, 1973, the bombing cut-off in Cambodia went into effect.

During the May vote, I spoke again with Dick Conlon. He was in a state of high elation.

Our most impatient, militant liberals never thought anything would really happen with our gradualist approach. They thought we were going too cautiously, too slowly. But we achieved a virtually unprecedented antiwar victory. We used all our most important reforms to turn the war issue around in the Congress. First, the monthly caucus enabled us to put the Democratic Party on the record against the war. Then, the Steering Committee permitted us to place the Democratic leadership in a position of supporting the antibombing amendment — which any of the Democratic conservative chairmen would have scuttled — and helped us pick up additional votes in the caucus and on the floor. Then, the record vote forced even the conservatives in the House to pay attention to the polls when they went to the floor to vote on the bombing.[12]

The potency of the reforms was vividly apparent in the fact that the Democrats gained fifty votes over the number they received on five antiwar ballots in the previous two years. Half of the fifty voters were the old-line regulars; half were new Democratic freshmen elected in 1972, many from the South. All cited public opinion and the caucus position as directly influencing their vote decision. The Republican antiwar votes (about 30 to 35) remained unchanged from the other years.[13] The reforms were instrumental in turning around the Democrats — though some party conservatives were probably ready to pull out of Cambodia because they no longer saw any national security interest in the bombing and abhorred the fiscal drain caused by the aerial raids.

This event was an abrupt departure from the old times, when progressives would merely have offered a variety of resolutions against the bombing which would have quickly died in committee; or, if by accident, had some reached the floor, the leadership would have chewed them up. But now the monthly caucus, the Steering Committee, and the recorded vote were three instruments reformers used to maximize their collective will in the House. On an issue like the Cambodian bombing, the combination of the three was unchallengeable.

Furthermore, by early 1973, inspired by Chairman Burton and a 1972 DSG task force led by Representative Jonathan B. Bingham (New York), in turn, backed up by the second Hansen Committee, the DSG began to pass a series of other reforms that gave liberals new authority in the House. What the changes did were to further centralize party decisions in the caucus and in the Speaker — the two party institutions most responsive to the national Democrats — and drastically clip the wings of the committee barons, who were least responsive to national policies. Thus, the Speaker got new powers to select Democrats for committees. He became, along with the Majority Leader and the caucus chairman, an ex-officio member of the Democratic Committee on Committees, the group that made all assignments for Democrats. The Speaker also got more authority to schedule legislation (a power generally granted to chairmen) and control policy (in naming all the members of the Steering Committee).

On the other hand, the caucus (in which the DSG more and more achieved majorities) got the power to confirm or reject by secret vote the chairman of every committee — a change that theoretically made seniority only one of several factors weighing in a congressman's designation. Also, the majority of the Democrats on any committee now had the power to form their own minicaucus and to determine the subcommittee budgets, its chairmen, and powers. Finally, the chairmen were now less free to work in secrecy, since other new rules permitted the press and public to sit in on the drafting sessions. Nor could chairmen any longer freely use the so-called "closed rule." This arcane device had enabled certain committees to disallow floor amendments by members of their own party and thereby assure that a particular committee's bill would be the only one the House considered.

Most reformers were thunderstruck. Nothing in the limited actions taken by the DSG in the past, or in the immovable nature of the House, or in any of Duberstein's most brashly optimistic *New Democrat* columns, would have prepared the progressives for the avalanche of changes that the DSG finally forced through in early 1973. I spoke with David Broder, the shrewd political writer for the Washington *Post* and an observer of Congress for years, about the remarkable upheaval. He said that these reforms

> are the biggest change in American government in the eighteen years I've been in Washington. The teller vote reform, for instance, makes it easier for Democratic liberals to organize around issues. The strengthened caucus and the larger role for the elected party leadership have given Democrats as a whole a new sense of party responsibility and given more input to all members over the decisions on the floor. Lastly, the changes have reduced the right of the individual chairmen to negotiate privately on legislation without any accountability to the majority sentiments of the party's members.[14]

These changes seemed to have happened for a variety of reasons, all of which the DSG used to advantage: first, Burton's recruitment policies, and then the 1972 congressional elections, which produced, by DSG's own count, an additional twenty-five to forty new reform legislators; second, the conversion of Albert and O'Neill to reform; third, "Nixon was the key," according to Broder, "by his contemptuous treatment of Congress on impoundment, spending, war powers, et cetera. Congressional moderates and liberals wanted to retake control of the House from Nixon";[15] fourth, the outrage over the Christmas bombing, which stiffened the spines of most Democrats against the House status quo; fifth, the second Hansen Committee's report, stitched together by a group of moderate Democrats over a two-year period, which made many of the DSG proposals acceptable to party regulars; and, finally, pressure from a host of good government organizations like Common Cause, and the Coalition for Congressional Reform, a group founded by Stewart Mott, which effectively publicized the issues outside the House.

Then, at the close of 1974, the DSG, swollen by the seventy-five progressive Democrats elected in the congressional elections in November, put an end to the remaining vestiges of the ancien régime in the House. In a December caucus of three days, the DSG forced the rigidly conservative Ways and Means Committee to break up into at least five subcommittees, restricting the chairman's once broad sway; the DSG majority also removed from the same committee the power to make committee assignments for all Democrats and placed it in its year-old creation, the Steering and Policy Committee. The caucus also voted itself to elect the heads of the twelve subcommittees on the other most powerful committee in the House, the Appropriations Committee. In addition, the caucus gave the Speaker the right to nominate all the members of the House Rules Committee, the central switchboard for legislation in the House. Finally, the caucus ordered that no party member could serve as chairman of two major committees simultaneously. These major shifts of power to the caucus and to the Speaker dramatically dissolved what little autocratic authority still remained to conservative Democratic chairmen under the seniority system. The party's power now gravitated to the Speaker and the policy committee, both of which were responsive to the active caucus of the majority party.

However, the caucus was unsuccessful in setting either an age limit or a term limit on committee chairmen, or making the Whip's office, the third-ranking leadership post, presently appointed by the Speaker and Majority Leader, elective. The caucus also did not bring much fresh order to the confusion of authority still existing between committees.

The DSG, through this cascade of reforms, became an unprecedented power in the House. Once an outcast, it was now a leader. Progressives, for the first time in decades, were better organized than the Dixiecrats. And the reforms very rapidly began to penetrate throughout the House. The swiftest and most immediate change was the secret vote on committee chairmen. It was the first time that progressives actually had the power to oust calcified chairmen. The veteran liberals in the House with whom I discussed the secret vote regarded this change as potentially the most significant. John Culver (Iowa), the husky, erudite chairman of the DSG after Burton, theorized that the vote was a

> nonviolent doctrine at work. People are going to cast their ballots not necessarily on whether a chairman is conservative or liberal, but whether he is fair to the others on the committee and whether he is responsive to the national party. The average chairman realizes that if he wins by a small margin in the caucus, that judgment will go back to his constituency, to his newspapers, and may even stimulate a primary contest or convince a member to retire. This will make a chairman less independent of the caucus and more responsive. It's really a change in attitude.[16]

Tip O'Neill, the bulky, foxy Majority Leader from Massachusetts, sitting in the most powerful post any DSG member has ever held, observed with a knowing nod of his head: "I used to feel that the House had slid into a position where the chairmen were all-powerful. Chairmen began to think they knew everything. After many years of ruling, they developed into dictators. Now power has been spread out. Chairmen realize they have to report to the caucus. Guys who used to behave autocratically are far more willing to listen to the wishes of the House leadership."[17] O'Neill was also happy to fortify the leadership's influence over the wayward chairmen through the caucus.

156

At first, however, the reform did not seem to have any effect. As Congressman Robert Drinan, a blunt-spoken DSG member from Massachusetts, caustically noted in *The Nation*: after the reform's enactment, all the chairmen had been overwhelmingly confirmed. Opposition ballots averaged only 11 percent. "Some progressives hailed it initially as a landmark but on reflection came to realize that it's pretty difficult to have much of an election between someone and no one . . . Actually the processes were designed to extend and embrace the power of the powerful and to confirm the powerlessness of those who expected only to sit and wait." Drinan added ominously what one freshman liberal had told him, " 'a system has been devised by which I can be denied a chairmanship six or eight years from now.' "[18]

But Drinan overstated his case, as was clear in January 1975, when the remarkable Ninety-Fourth Congress deposed three established chairmen by caucus vote. Drinan still had the fear — which Mike Duberstein also had long possessed — that the House system was hopelessly rigged against the liberals. Actually, the DSG reform was not designed to knock out automatically the most hopeless conservative chairmen, but simply to enforce more equity on a previously nonregulated industry. The DSG was using a gradualist approach, chipping away at the granite walls piece by piece, moving slowly toward a breakthrough, but not trying for instant results.

Nonetheless, Drinan's caveat could not be completely dismissed, however successful the reform. One wondered whether the DSG had a monitoring system capable of checking on the changes, improving and strengthening them, and discarding them when they no longer worked. This called into question the DSG's fundamental strength. Since it was just a creature of the liberals, labor Democrats, progressive moderates, and big-city regulars in Congress, it could only be as weak or formidable as they were. In short, did the DSG have the power to prevent the reforms' being turned against its own interest?

This was a delicate topic, I found, one about which seasoned reformers had thought long and hard. Richard Bolling, a member of the DSG, grumbled to me: "Reform is a dynamic process. There is no safeguard against the ineptitude of the majority. The DSG must realize this. Every good reform can later become a vice. People must keep on working to perfect the process. You can't make democracy a perfect thing. You can't institutionalize fairness."[19] Dick Conlon, ever at the center of the maelstrom, was bothered by the fear of a loss of vigilance, or a lapse in judgment, or a mood that took the reforms for granted: "All the reforms may work in the end, but they boil down to a determination on the part of the majority to exercise its power. The DSG is the majority. We know now that we have the mechanisms. However, if we don't get ourselves together, nothing will happen. The reformers can bring the horse to water, but if the horse doesn't want to drink, it doesn't make much difference which reforms pass."[20]

In a sense, the DSG was not totally in control of its own fate in these matters. There were still many areas in the House over which the DSG and its collection of reforms and rules had no influence. The DSG could not yet dent every level of the seniority system; it could not overrule the House leadership; and it could not always tell chairmen how to run their committees. Any of these power centers might bend the reforms to other purposes if they wished. At this time, the DSG could at best put up limited resistance.

Still, most of these areas were no longer as forbidding or threatening to the progressives as they once were. For example, seniority was perhaps less of a threat than it had been in the fifties and sixties. The reforms of the 1970s had crimped the institution a little. The domination of chairmanships by Southerners had also dropped steadily through attrition in the sixties and early seventies. There was not a single legislator from the original Confederate states in the Speakership, Majority Leadership, or Whip's office after Hale Boggs's death in 1972. And seniority was now helping DSG members who had served in the House for over a decade move into posts on powerful committees.

The committee system, though, was still very troubling for the DSG. The chairmen could plan their own strategy on legislation — what to send to the floor, when to schedule votes, and so on. There was also overlapping of jurisdiction between committees. For instance, to pass a bill to open up the highway trust fund to mass transit, five major committees had to hold hearings. Thus, committees were still an obstacle course for reform ideas.

The House leadership also was a mixed bag — with not enough power to coordinate Democratic policy among the committee chairmen, but with just enough power to confuse legislative strategy. In April 1973, the Democrats proposed a price rollback during a nationwide meat boycott that grew out of the largest jump in wholesale prices in twenty-two years. Since this issue emerged after the passage of the DSG reforms, the Speaker had available to him the same weapons he had used to pass the anti-Cambodian bombing legislation — the policy organ, the party caucus, and the recorded vote. But Albert did not bother to write a complete scenario. The Democrats fumbled the issue and the Nixon administration got its own legislation enacted. Albert Hunt of the *Wall Street Journal* pinned the fiasco on "the bungling of the House Democrats. Without their political ineptitude, it's doubtful the administration could ever have won its victory."[21]

These were some of the variables, then, over which the DSG had no real influence. Still, within the rather elastic bounds of the House rules, the DSG had some power to impress its views on the Democrats, providing that two conditions were always met: that its membership continued to be robust, and that its stewardship continued to be capable. The first condition was fulfilled in the late sixties and early seventies. In the elections of 1968, 1970, 1972, and 1974, the DSG picked up progressive members. This was partly because crusty elders were retiring in droves to take advantage of the excellent congressional pension plans, and others were being eliminated by primaries, desire to run for other offices, or by death; and it was partly because of the anti-incumbency mood following the Watergate scandals. The DSG met the second condition well, too. The organization seemed to have a facility for attracting able chairmen. The study group elected diligent, adept, and intelligent members of the reform faith in the House — Frank Thompson, James O'Hara, Donald Fraser, Phillip Burton, John Culver, Tom Foley. With its high-powered back-up staff, the DSG remained, as much by necessity as default, the most influential progressive interest group in House affairs.

The DSG, in addition, maintained its stature among House members because it seldom sought publicity for itself. All the people associated with the study group, particularly the staff, deliberately deflated DSG's role in the great reform upheavals, in the Cambodian bombing reversal, and in other contemporary battles. The unstated credo by which the DSG worked was that its effectiveness lay behind the scenes. The belief was that, if it began to appear in the headlines, the Democratic leadership might take steps to restrain it. And House conservatives might deem it wise to set up a strong counterblock.

But for all of the DSG's adeptness since 1969, there were disturbing intangibles that clouded its future. The DSG's core followers in the early seventies had never risen to more than forty or fifty, though the DSG had a complete muster of over 160 members. Would that be enough to carry forward the progressive cause? There were also chronic money problems — the DSG was entirely dependent on contributions for dues and office salaries from its own congressmen. Would they continue to donate? Furthermore, there was a dangerous Balkanization process at work in the House. There were now a Rural Caucus, a Black Caucus, a New England Caucus, a Conservative Democratic Caucus, and a Democratic Moderates Caucus. Many in the DSG were members of one or more of these other groups. Would their double memberships dilute their loyalty to the DSG?

When asked, Dick Conlon insisted that as long as the DSG's philosophy was being implemented through structural reforms he believed the reforms and the DSG would be protected:

> First, I believe in the concept of party government. The party caucus should be the controlling factor. It should be able to instruct the chairmen and committees on the party's stances. It can do this now. The results of the caucus may not be the liberal position, but neither will they be the conservative position. They at least will be the party position.
>
> Second, I believe in the concept of inside-outside pressure groups to force change in Congress. The outside groups can

raise the issues generally and build a fire in a congressman's district. The inside groups then develop the strategy, the details of the reforms, and play the whip's role. But the insiders can't move without the outsiders' exertions. Our group is still in the position to link up with outside pressures to change things internally.

Finally, DSG Democrats have the power to employ all the tools that now exist to control the direction of the Democratic Party, to build a party consensus on liberal legislation, and to prevent committee chairmen from distorting national legislation toward conservative ends. The question really is: will the DSG liberals continue to act forcefully?[22]

Conlon's thesis, of course, is tested anew every year. A great struggle, for instance, broke out in 1974 over a new collection of reforms, brought forward by the so-called Bolling Committee, a ten-man select committee headed by Congressman Richard Bolling to untie the jurisdictional knots and legislative tangles between House committees, cut back or actually abolish some committees, and redistribute representatives among committees. The idea was originally proposed by John Culver. The DSG, oddly enough, was split over the Bolling package. Some reformers, like Burton, whose own committees would lose substantial powers under the reorganization plan, argued that the changes strengthened the present structure; others, like Culver, regarded them as indispensable at a time when polls showed Congress at an all-time low in public repute. The ADA and Common Cause sided with Culver. The DSG as a body took no position.

It did not seem that Bolling's proposals would hurt the progressives. The DSG reforms in the early seventies were of such a fundamental nature that a series of committee reorganizations, some good, some bad, which Bolling proposed, could hardly affect the changed power arrangements of the DSG very much and might on balance rationalize the House structure, thereby making it more vulnerable to systematic DSG probes. However, the Bolling proposal was temporarily put aside in favor of some more moderate changes proposed by a third Hansen Committee set up by the caucus.

To the House leadership, the progressives had nonetheless arrived as a political power. Tip O'Neill told me he regarded the DSG as

> a strong adjunct to the Democratic Party. I've been a member of the DSG since its infancy. I have helped them financially. I have sold tickets for their benefits. I have helped them with their staff payrolls. Most of the House reforms started with them. At first the Democratic establishment had a lot of animosity toward the DSG, but that has died away. There is an aura now in the House of passing the power around to everyone through reforms. The younger fellows now have a chance. The day of the strong Speaker is over. The ball game's changed. We are all creatures of the caucus. The DSG represents, in all of this, the philosophy of the majority of the Democratic Party. The DSG is sort of a watchdog of our politics. The House leadership always cooperates with the DSG and consults with them.[23]

I pressed O'Neill on the DSG's influence in caucus votes, where it held a majority. Would a DSG consensus automatically mean its success on any vote? O'Neill frowned at the notion and muttered, "We won't let that happen here."[24] The leadership, it seemed quite apparent, would listen to the DSG, but did not plan to take orders from it.

Nonetheless, the DSG as a bloc in the House has now emerged as an idea bank, an agitator for reform, a de facto conscience of the Democratic Party. As Donald Fraser, the quietly intellectual Minnesotan (once DSG chairman, once ADA chairman, and once chairman of the old McGovern Commission on Party Structure and Delegate Selection) remarked in a discussion about the DSG's unique role in Congress:

> The power of the DSG has today become considerable. First of all, in the House there are four hundred and thirty-five members all doing their own thing. So ad hoc efforts, committees, or groups like the DSG are the only way to get people together around issues. Second, the DSG's role is to take the lead on an issue. It gets people thinking and then Congress starts thinking about the issue. Finally, when an issue is approved by the DSG, and thus is shown to be acceptable to the broad range of progressives in the party, it has a decided impact on the party and Congress as a whole.[25]

The DSG has, in short, made progressivism respectable in the House. It has built up an autonomous liberal coalition that can take part in the bargaining process in Congress. It has offered the reform movements a new way of plugging into the Congress. It has made a once hide-bound institution responsive to the new sentiment for change rising throughout the United States.

7 ☆

The Minorities Rise Up

FOUR DISTINCT MINORITIES — the Chicanos, the Puerto Ricans, the Indians, and the Gays — burst into American politics in the late sixties and early seventies, and significantly enlarged the compass of the reform movement. Each agitated for recognition in society, inundated the public with leaflets, picketed the government, heckled the opposition, created a voting bloc, and prospered to some extent as an interest group in the progressive wings of both the Republican and Democratic parties.

We at *The New Democrat* always wished we had given better exposure to these awakening movements. However, none of the four had a cohesive reform organization (similar to the New Democratic Coalition or the Congressional Black Caucus or the National Women's Political Caucus) that was accessible to coverage. Instead, because all four groups had special constituencies with unique cultural backgrounds and mores far removed from conventional political life, their members tended to congregate around single leaders or around a series of diverse coalitions and work only indirectly in reform life.

My first consciousness about the Chicano community, for instance, came not from elected officials but rather through Cesar Chavez and the boycott of nonunion lettuce and grapes in the early sixties. The struggle of Chavez's union, the United Farm Workers, over pitiful wages and primitive living conditions awakened many social activists in the country. Chavez rapidly became the most luminous and influential leader among the Chicanos and retained his prestige among his people even when the Teamsters muscled in on the California vineyards in the seventies and persuaded most of the growers to sign labor contracts with them.

The elected Chicano leaders, however, had grown in importance by 1972, and they made a heavy imprint in the McGovern campaign. In the fall of 1972, Milt Gwirtzman, the coordinator of speechwriters, asked me to prepare a speech for McGovern to give at Espanola, New Mexico. McGovern wanted to strengthen his ties with the Chicanos of the American Southwest. In the past decades, the Spanish-speaking peoples of the United States, although they turned out lightly, voted in spectacular proportions for the Democratic candidates, sometimes up to 90 percent. And about 5.1 million Mexican-Americans lived in the Southwest — in New Mexico, Arizona, California, Colorado, and Texas — many of them representing swing votes in close presidential elections.

From the start, I found that the Washington McGovern headquarters was having trouble formulating a specific position on the Chicanos. During the California primary, Mc-Govern had committed himself to a ten-point plan for the Chicano community, which included a pledge to hire Spanish-speaking individuals for governmental posts "in reasonable relationship" to their presence in the population. This language was not unfamiliar — it was borrowed directly from the wording of the McGovern guidelines. But it was instantly plagued by the same infirmity that bedeviled the party reforms: does "reasonable relationship" constitute a quota or merely a goal toward which all Democrats should work? By now, incorrectly or not, the answer didn't matter anymore, for the words flapped like red flags in the political breezes and signaled only one thing to the voters: quotas. It was clear that McGovern's broad commitment was going to have to be altered to conform with the current antiquota sentiment.

However, the young Chicanos on the McGovern staff, who had labored for months for McGovern in the field and were now in the Washington headquarters looking out for their political interests, were incensed that McGovern might step back from his California promises at Espanola. A number of them came to me, in despair, about the McGovern address. I went to great lengths to explain the quota controversy, which had billowed through the campaign far out of proportion to its real importance as an issue. They agreed to sit down and thrash things out, but they did not agree that McGovern should retreat one bit from his pledges to the Mexican-American community.

Just at this time, Richard Cohen, our coordinator for Jewish Affairs, who had gotten wind of the Espanola speech, came to me in some distress. He insisted that I arrange a meeting between him and the Chicanos on the staff. He was anxious that McGovern's speech say nothing, even in the form of a hint, about quotas, which were objectionable to Jewish voters because they had been used for years to exclude Jews from law schools, government jobs, and other professions. He was agreeable, he said, to trying to work out with the Chicanos new statements on employment and hiring, reflecting a commitment to affirmative action.

Amidst this cacophony of voices, the administrative aide to New Mexico's Chicano senator, Joseph Montoya, suddenly put in my hands a prepared speech for McGovern to use at Espanola. Montoya's contributions were actually a toned-down version of the twenty-four demands presented by the "Latino Caucus" at the Democratic National Convention — a list of requests on civil rights legislation, economic aid, and job hiring that Chicanos and Puerto Ricans and Cubans had put together for Miami. Montoya's suggestions included hazy references to the delicate topic of job quotas.

By this time, I was cutting and splicing, arranging meetings, canceling conferences, attempting to bridge all sorts of gaps and misunderstandings, trying to appease various Chicano leaders, and gradually putting into shape a speech that would reflect all the various requests without mentioning quotas. After getting general acquiescence to the language on affirmative action — although some Chicanos still protested any pullback from the California covenants — I finally completed a version of a "Chicano manifesto" and, a week before Espanola, I sent it to the campaign plane.

I never heard about my proposals again. McGovern gave a completely different talk at Espanola, stressing an "agenda" for "Spanish-surnamed Americans." According to Paul Wieck of *The New Republic,* who was present at Espanola, McGovern

> promised "full funding" of bilingual educations, efforts to assure justice, economic opportunities and full participation in the nation's political life — all items of general acceptability. On hiring policies, McGovern side-stepped any statement that could

be interpreted as a "quota." He condemned Nixon's 16-point program for the Spanish-speaking on the grounds that "only 2.9 percent of Civil Service employees are Latinos" and "the majority are in the lower grades" while only 45 persons are in grades "where policy and priority are made." He then promised "to remedy gross under-representation and insure Latino and other minorities input in program funding and development," terminology his supporters can privately say means the same thing as a "quota."[1]

Later, in Washington, some of the Chicanos on the staff stopped by to see me, wondering what McGovern had said and asking me if I could give them a copy of his speech. I gladly dug out the last few Xeroxes of my own draft and gave them all copies, explaining in an aside that McGovern had used only "a little of my material." They took my drafts but were very displeased to learn that I had no copies of the address McGovern had actually delivered. Nobody in Washington had ever received one. In the days following, I looked assiduously for a draft of McGovern's Espanola speech or for a press report on it. In fact, I never discovered an original version of the candidate's talk even after the campaign, when I rummaged through an abandoned speech file cabinet. The sole notice of it I found (besides the New Mexican newspapers) was Paul Wieck's coverage.

Wieck's account, however, was most perceptive, not simply for the general report on his speech, but also for his analysis of McGovern's muddled efforts to close ranks with the Chicano leaders in the Southwest. There was, Wieck wrote, a "constant hassle between the local McGovern people and his national staff during his brief stay in New Mexico. One got the impression that no one's really in charge. In New Mexico, Montoya has been named to head the campaign; however, the local McGovern people did not include him on the list of dignitaries to greet McGovern when he arrived at the airport."[2]

Montoya, it later turned out, was not offended by this disorganization. He had successfully assembled a crowd of 20,000 for McGovern, the largest audience to hear the candidate on his first solid week of campaigning after his nomination. It drew Indians, Anglos [the English-speaking population], and "small farmers and ranchers," Wieck wrote, "with names like Chacon and Baca whose ancestors had followed the conquistadores to northern New Mexico nearly 400 years ago . . ."[3]

Montoya was a crucial link to the Chicano community. He was from an old "patron" family, a member of the social elite of the state of New Mexico. Though he looked rather ineffectual during the Watergate hearings, he was powerful on his home grounds, and well regarded as a Chicano who had "made it." Montoya was an assimilationist, too, rather than a separatist, and spoke for the moderates in the Chicano communities. He was also capable of saying in anger on the Senate floor, as he did in 1972: "At a very minimum, demeaning characterizations of Hispanos must be removed from publicly licensed facilities and airwaves . . . Outrageous discrimination existing in higher levels of Government employment must be removed instantly. The Civil Service Commission and administration have the power to act and should immediately do so . . . Chicano communities demand political power and equal opportunity. If it is not forthcoming, there will be terrible violence, like it or not."[4]

There existed few other political movements among the Chicanos outside the regular Democratic Party to which reformers like McGovern paid attention. On balance, most were militant, had spotty support among the Chicano communities, and generally opposed Democratic candidates — partly because Democrats cut into the strength of their own causes. For example, in New Mexico in the late sixties, a Mexican-American named Reies Lopez Tijerina crusaded to reclaim old Spanish land grants, which, he charged, had been illegally stolen by the Anglos. He actually made a citizen's arrest of some local officials to impress on the public his seriousness of purpose. His activities attracted a lot of notoriety, and for a moment Tijerina threatened to found a Chicano party to oppose Montoya and the Democrats. But he was arrested for his protests and his movement soon petered out.

A more successful political movement was La Raza Unida. It started in 1970 in Texas as an electoral rebellion of poor Mexican-Americans against the powerful, land-owning Anglo families. There were then twenty-six counties in the state where Chicanos were the majority of the population; three-quarters of them were living at or below the poverty line. About twenty-five Anglo families controlled most of the land and wealth. In April 1970, José Angel Gutierrez, a fiery Mexican-American leader, sparked a revolt over the Crystal City school system, which was overwhelmingly Chicano but which had traditionally selected Anglos as cheerleaders and homecoming queens — and he and two other Chicanos won seats on the school board. This small stone cast into the sea of apathetic Chicanos in the Southwest sent ripples everywhere; within three years, Gutierrez' party, La Raza Unida, won local elections in other Texas counties and spread into New Mexico, California, and Colorado.[5]

However, Gutierrez' outlook was basically sectarian. In 1972, when Sissy Farenthold challenged Dolph Briscoe, a Democratic conservative, for governor, La Raza Unida put up its own candidate and heaped scorn on Farenthold for not withdrawing in his favor. Farenthold narrowly lost to Briscoe in the primary. In a state where liberals seldom triumph and therefore need every vote they can round up, La Raza Unida's decision helped doom Farenthold's candidacy. As Paul Wieck commented: "This defection of an important militant group from the main struggle for control of Texas [leaves] the liberal coalition at the mercy of the old-style 'money' politicians who flourish in Spanish-speaking communities across the Southwest."[6]

McGovern himself had an ambivalent attitude toward La Raza Unida, a reflection of the uncertainty felt by many Democratic liberals toward Gutierrez. Just before McGovern's arrival in Espanola, his headquarters issued a statement in the candidate's name, condemning the shooting of a La Raza Unida delegate at a filling station in southern New Mexico as a "senseless act of insanity." By the time McGovern reached the state, however, some of the New Mexican Chicanos warned him that all the facts about the incident weren't yet known and that they were concerned about prejudging a case about to go on trial. So McGovern, the next morning, told the press that the telegram had been sent by a member of his staff without his knowledge, and he retracted the statement. The La Raza Unida people were outraged by McGovern's retreat and threatened retaliation in Texas. Some McGovern strategists, however — and, indeed, a number of other Chicano liberals I spoke to — were not greatly concerned about La Raza's fulminations. Rumors had reached campaign tacticians that the Nixon administration had directed Federal OEO funds and small business loans toward La Raza Unida's leaders in the hope of keeping them neutral or not publicly anti-Nixon. (These rumors were later confirmed at the Watergate hearings.) It was felt, by McGovern's staff, that there was little or nothing the candidate could do to defuse the hostility of La Raza Unida.

For the most part, the other political organizations among the Chicanos were strongly liberal, promoting the candidacies of progressive Spanish-speaking brethren all over the Southwest. In Texas, the most active group was the Political Association of Spanish Organizations (PASO); in California, the Mexican-American Political Association (MAPA). In all five Southwestern states, many Chicanos worked through local branches of the National GI Forum, the Mexican-American veteran group formed after World War II to encourage Chicanos to run for election.

In 1972, in fact, the Chicano awakening was considerable. The California delegation to the Democratic Convention in that year was 17 percent Mexican-American; and the overall Spanish-speaking presence in Miami was four times larger than it had been in Chicago. Though most television viewers were not accustomed to seeing so many Chicanos at a political gathering — and some may have been frightened by the militancy of the Chicano activists — the nation understood that the Spanish-speaking element had now become a significant element in American politics.

Yet all this activity — the Chicano presence at the Democratic Convention, which the reforms helped to generate, the growth of Chicano caucuses throughout the Southwest, the publicity and crowds that greeted McGovern's appearance at

Espanola, the development of the Chicano agenda — made little difference to the election. In 1972, the Spanish-speaking vote for the Democratic candidate dropped sharply and increased for the Republicans. Nixon in 1968 had received 5 percent of the Spanish-speaking ballots; four years later, his proportion shot up to 27 percent. In the Southwest, Nixon got 43 percent of the Chicano vote in New Mexico, 26 percent in California, and 20 percent in Texas. The turnabout was devastating.[7] This change in voting habits obviously pleased the Republicans. The Democrats became painfully aware that they could not neglect the Chicanos in the future.

The Puerto Ricans were less active than the Chicanos. In the main, the reason was geography — Puerto Ricans had their own isle and did not think of the United States as a permanent homeland. Most Puerto Ricans in coming to the States wanted only to save up enough money to return to their island and settle down with their families. As Congressman Herman Badillo, the only Puerto Rican in Congress, once commented, "The Puerto Ricans who come to the States are the poor ones, the unskilled, the uneducated. If they weren't poor, they wouldn't leave Puerto Rico. Once they make it here, they return home."[8]

This perpetual inflow-outflow created a chronic political ambivalence among Puerto Ricans and made for an immensely unstable voting bloc. There were 1.4 million Puerto Ricans living in New York City alone in 1970. Puerto Ricans also inhabited cities like Hartford, Boston, Miami, and Chicago, and worked in rural areas in New Jersey and Connecticut. Where there were local political machines, as in sections of New York City, Puerto Ricans overwhelmingly registered and voted Democratic. Where livelihoods were only transient, as in the tobacco fields around Hartford, they rarely registered or participated in elections.

Many bright, able Puerto Rican liberals were caught up, without really wishing to be, in the immensely complicated relationship between the United States and Puerto Rico. Marco Rigau, Jr., for example, a classmate of mine from law school days, lived two separate political lives in the United States and on the island. A brash, incisive young lawyer, overflowing with charm and ambition, he was active in Robert Kennedy's senatorial career in New York, working for a time in Kennedy's New York office. He then returned to the island and plunged into the Popular Party, the movement begun in the 1940s by one of the great figures of Puerto Rican history, Luis Muñoz Marín. Muñoz' party helped to establish Puerto Rico as a "commonwealth," a status which conferred on all Puerto Ricans American citizenship and the duty to serve in the United States Armed Forces — but also ordained that no Puerto Rican had to pay federal income taxes or had the right to vote in presidential elections. In 1972, the Popular Party was hoping to defeat the ruling Statehood Party, which had ties to the mainland Republican Party. The Popular Party, with links to the Democratic Party, nominated as its candidate for governor Hernandez-Colon, a young protégé of Muñoz' and a leader in the commonwealth's legislature. Rigau became an aide-de-camp for Colon. Colon swept the Popular Party back to the governorship.

Rigau, along with Colon, supported McGovern for the Democratic nomination. Colon headed the Popular Party's delegation to the Democratic Convention at Miami. It struck me as a bit anomalous, as I told Rigau at Miami, that Puerto

Rico should send delegates to Miami to choose the Democratic nominee but, on their return to Puerto Rico, could not vote for the same man for the presidency. Rigau replied that most Popular Party members feared if Puerto Ricans once participated in American elections they would begin to demand statehood — a step that Muñoz Marín, Hernandez-Colon, and most Puerto Rican leaders opposed because they believed statehood would jeopardize, perhaps cripple forever, the fragile economy and political stability of Puerto Rico.

After the election, in 1973, Colon appointed Rigau head of the Migration Division of Puerto Rico on the mainland, headquartered in New York City. The office oversaw the conditions of Puerto Ricans working in the United States. Rigau, a person of strong ideals, moved into the job with the utmost seriousness and began to investigate the lives of Puerto Rican migrant workers in places like Connecticut and New Jersey. To his disgust and indignation, he discovered unsanitary living conditions, illegally low wages, concentration camp discipline, all enforced upon defenseless Puerto Rican migrants. He found out that the American companies were not complying with the labor contracts signed with the Puerto Rican Labor Department, which promised pay scales, camp sanitation, and decent working conditions for the Puerto Rican employees.

Rigau, striking out in his own flamboyant style, tried to arouse public anger over the exploitation of the Puerto Rican laborers. He called me one day, asking how he might best approach the New York newspapers, notoriously indifferent to Puerto Rican matters. After some calls and the intercessions of various intermediaries, the *New York Times* finally printed a piece on Rigau's struggle. In Puerto Rico, Rigau's adamant statements produced banner headlines all over the island. But his boss in Puerto Rico, the secretary of labor, frowned on the dispute; and when Governor Colon refused to back him up, Rigau resigned.

Rigau remained in New York for a time to write a book on the migrants and to participate in a study of the criminal justice system and its impact on Spanish-speaking citizens of New York. Such was his reputation among the Puerto Ricans in the city, and such was the size of the Puerto Rican voting bloc (in 1970, more than three-fifths of all Puerto Ricans in the United States lived in New York City), that a number of Puerto Rican and Democratic Party leaders tried to persuade him to give up his plans to return to the island and, instead, to run for the United States Congress. Rigau, at this point, had the choice of two worlds. He finally decided to go home and enter Puerto Rican politics.

Other influential Puerto Ricans decided to stay on the mainland. The foremost Puerto Rican leader was Representative Herman Badillo. He had grown up in New York City and was educated at CCNY and Brooklyn Law School. In 1969 and again in 1973, he almost won the Democratic primary for mayor. Both times, however, the New Democratic Coalition endorsed other candidates. In 1972, Badillo's endorsement and his symbolic position as a Puerto Rican leader were helpful to McGovern early in his campaign. In 1973, Badillo blasted the newly elected New York City mayor, Abe Beame, for not hiring enough Puerto Ricans in his administration after Beame had received the overwhelming majority of Puerto Rican votes in the election. Badillo's protest forced Beame to appoint more Puerto Ricans, although Beame took care to choose mostly those who were independent of Badillo.

Badillo, an intelligent and urbane man, filled a special niche in New York. He was a kind of one-man ethnic caucus, a pressure agent for Puerto Ricans in city and state affairs, an interpreter of the Spanish-speaking community to New Yorkers who did not understand the different culture or the language or the style of dress or the code of "macho." On the "Today Show," Badillo once tried to put Puerto Ricans in the context of the "universal" American experience:

> The problems of Puerto Ricans are not the problems of a particular situation, but of the whole country. The American cities are being abandoned and the Puerto Ricans are suffering along with the blacks and the poor whites. There is, besides, racism in United States life. If a Puerto Rican is white, he's treated as a white person. If he's a black Puerto Rican, he's treated as a black person. If he's mixed, he can be treated either way. The Puerto Rican question is the American question.[9]

Despite Badillo's presence — or perhaps because of it — the Puerto Ricans had not yet grasped their opportunity. They had relatively small numbers in the United States, an ambivalence about American politics, a cultural alienation, and a confinement to the New York area. Yet, in an era of fluid politics and deteriorating parties, some began to realize that a sophisticated, disciplined ethnic caucus could assume an influence beyond its numbers, particularly by exploiting the new reform guidelines in both parties.

The first signs of a new consciousness were evident in 1972. The Puerto Ricans in New York increased their representation on the state Democratic delegation from 2 percent in 1968 to 6 percent in 1972 in Miami. Many Puerto Ricans joined with the Chicanos and some Cubans to create the Latino Caucus at the 1972 convention. Later, they set up a formal Latino Caucus among committeemen and committeewomen at the

Democratic National Committee. Finally, in New York state, the handful of Puerto Rican legislators in the State Senate and Assembly combined in a caucus with the black legislators to influence policy. Unfortunately, blacks and Puerto Ricans did not work particularly well together in the neighborhoods, and the tensions between two groups that might have been natural allies weakened both of them. The real strength of Puerto Ricans in reform politics was still expressed through individuals like Badillo and local district leaders.

Even so, the Puerto Rican power was greater than that of the American Indians. The Indians numbered about 800,000 in the early 1970s, slightly over half the number of Puerto Ricans, though the Indian population had increased an estimated 50 percent since the 1960 census. Indians were widely dispersed around the country; half of them lived in the West and a quarter in the South, and the population as a whole was about evenly divided between cities and reservations. As a class of citizen, they tended to be very poor and very alienated. More shockingly, their suicide rate was one hundred times that of whites. Nevertheless, they were beginning to function as an ethnic bloc in the seventies.

In 1970, the Nixon administration had ended the policy of terminating reservations and assimilating all Indians into American society, proclaiming, instead, "self-determination without termination" as the government's policy. Nixon also began to Indianize the Indian Bureau of the Department of the Interior, which for years whites had run as a paternalistic operation. The Nixon changes had been preceded by an explosion in Indian consciousness in the late sixties. A series of books spurred a mood of reappraisal. Vine Deloria, Jr., a

Standing Rock Sioux and a former executive director of the National Congress of American Indians (NCAI) founded during World War II (in which 25,000 Indians served in United States forces), wrote *Custer Died for Your Sins* in 1969 and Dee Brown published *Bury My Heart at Wounded Knee* in 1971. An "underground" film, *Billy Jack*, captured the fancy of the counterculture and quickly moved above ground to become one of the most popular and profitable movies of all times — a tale of a proud, sensitive half-breed, a veteran of the Vietnam War, who returned to his tribal grounds and became involved in protecting a "free school" from harassment by rednecks in the American Southwest.

The Indians were also growing more nationalistic. The two oldest groups representing traditional Indian authority were beginning to speak out more vigorously for Indian rights. These were the NCAI, which lobbied for Indians in Washington, D.C., and the National Tribal Chairman's Association (NTCA), which included the chiefs of most of the Indian tribes. They were both being goaded to tougher positions by the radical American Indian Movement (AIM), composed mainly of urban Indians and founded in 1968. AIM had publicly denounced both the NCAI and the NTCA as tools of the anti-Indian white establishment.

AIM surged forward with the same militancy as the Student Non-Violent Coordinating Committee (SNCC) had in the midst of the black movement in the sixties. In 1972, AIM engineered a brief (and destructive) occupation of the Bureau of Indian Affairs and, in 1973, the well-publicized takeover of Wounded Knee. In late 1973, however, James Sterba of the *New York Times* wrote that all three Indian organizations now "appear more willing to cooperate than in the past.

Indian leaders attribute this in part to a heightened awareness of Indian issues on the reservations and a growing militancy, especially by young Indians, in the past year — for which AIM takes credit."[10] The possibility of a single political caucus for Indians dawned.

Political leaders, too, were beginning to recognize the existence of the Indians. One of the most outspoken was Robert Kennedy, who, as senator from New York, chaired extensive hearings into the poverty and anomie of the Indians, and during his brief campaign for the presidency in 1968 visited several Indian reservations. McGovern's Indian program, set forth during his campaign for the Democratic nomination in 1972, went further to meet the demands of militant Indians than anything offered by any previous candidate of either party. The Native American Lobby, an Indian lobby in Washington, stated:

> There are a great many similarities between President Nixon's and Senator McGovern's positions. Both agree on self-determination, contracting, hiring, and more money all around. It is interesting though that each has a dramatically opposite position on Urban Indians. McGovern recognizes that Indians do not lose their identity if they move off the reservation. To Nixon an Indian must be on trust land. McGovern senses that a moral obligation was established when the government policy was to support and encourage Indian migration to the cities. Urban Indians, almost half of the total Indian population, get a better deal with McGovern . . . no other Democratic candidate has matched his record.[11]

McGovern had evolved his position through the years as a result of his own experiences with the Indians of his home state, South Dakota — the state, of course, where the Wounded Knee drama unfolded soon after the 1972 election.

McGovern's Senate resolution, introduced first in 1969, called for a self-determination policy and a halt to the termination of reservations. Indians, McGovern declared, must be able to secure for themselves every freedom enjoyed by all other Americans, to manage and control their own lives, their individual affairs and tribal policies. This meant handing over to the Indians administration of their schools, providing job training in or near reservations, setting up legal and technical assistance for poor and small tribes, and creating an Indian-directed and -staffed Office of Indian Affairs in the White House.

Not unexpectedly, this record soon convinced five of the seven recorded Indian delegates and three alternates to the 1972 Democratic Convention in Miami to pledge themselves to McGovern.[12] Curiously, none of the Indian delegates to Miami came from the Southwest, where 35 percent of the Indians lived; they were a mixture of urban Indians from states like Massachusetts and Minnesota, and rural Indians from the Plains states, like Iowa, South Dakota, and Wyoming.

After his nomination, McGovern made his first foray to win Indian support on his trip to Espanola, New Mexico. This state, with the fourth largest U.S. Indian populace, was a new arena for Indian activism. For years, politicians in the Southwest had gerrymandered election districts to divide Indians on the reservations from their brothers in the cities in such a way as to deprive Indians of their ability to act as a bloc. Now, as Paul Wieck observed in *The New Republic* in 1972, "Arizona and New Mexico have large concentrations of Indians whose political awareness has been growing and now are 'up for grabs' this year. For the first time, large numbers of Indians from some of the culturally conservative tribes (such as the Pueblos up and down the Rio Grande) are registering to vote."[13] The local McGovern organization worked energetically through tribal leaders on the reservation to get Indians on the rolls.

In this period, however, tensions were bubbling up in New Mexico between some of the Indian tribes and the Chicanos in the Democratic Party, prompting a number of Indian leaders to turn Republican. Wieck noted:

> Relations between the Spanish-speaking and the Indians aren't always the best when it comes to politics. Not only was it the Spanish (rather than the Anglos) who conquered them a few centuries back, but the Spanish-speaking politicians are reluctant to surrender any of their political power to the awakening Indians. Now a few Indian leaders are Republican. A struggle is going on in Sandoval County, New Mexico, the home county of Senator Montoya of New Mexico. There, the Indians are half the population. They're registering and teaming up with the Anglo minority to wrest control from the Spanish to the embarrassment of Montoya (his brother is one of the targets of the new coalition).[14]

The strife between the Indians and the Chicanos was troubling to the McGovern organization, which still sought a sizeable share of the new Indian vote on the basis of McGovern's sweeping legislative agenda for the Indians and because of the identification of many Indians with past Democratic policies, like the Office of Economic Opportunity's antipoverty programs, the only federally funded enterprises that Indians ran themselves. McGovern's own campaign staff also included a few prominent Indian advisors, notably La Donna Harris, the Indian wife of former Senator Fred Harris of Oklahoma. But the Indian vote in the 1972 election was not statistically significant to McGovern.

The staying power of Indian activism amidst the rough and

tumble and insensitivity of white politics is now undoubtedly problematic in the later seventies. Indian tribes remain so scattered around the country and so fragmented among 300 different nations that it is almost impossible for them to sustain a single political bloc. The poverty, illiteracy, and despair that permeate most reservations still make many Indians apathetic about voting or joining political organizations. And the most poignant and haunting problem is that, when Indians do confront U.S. politics, they have to consider whether to give up their separate tribal societies to engage in political action within the American context. There does not appear to be any position in between.

Yet many Indians continue to seek a peculiarly native form of political self-determination in the United States. As Martin Waldron reported in the *New York Times* in 1974: "From coast to coast, Indians are expressing a deep longing for independence, with each tribe able to make and enforce its own laws. The Indians, however, expect the United States to continue paying all or most of the costs of the tribes."[15] For the Navajo tribe, for example, the largest in the nation — 140,000 — self-determination has meant the desire to carve its own state out of Arizona, New Mexico, and Utah. To fortify its new sense of political identity, it financed in 1974 a $50,000 voter-registration drive to register 70,000 Navajo Indians to defeat Senator Barry Goldwater, who championed the Hopi Indians in their land dispute with the Navajo. Although the future of the Indian voting constituency in liberal politics seems uncertain, stirrings in tribes like the Navajo suggest that an Indian political movement is still possible.

The other constituency that sprang into public notice in this period was the homosexuals, or, as they had begun to style themselves, the Gays. The Gays came into public consciousness as an organized group in 1969, when a police raid on a homosexual bar in Greenwich Village set off a series of demonstrations by homosexuals against the New York City Police Department. This uprising, in turn, led to the creation of the Gay Activists Alliance (GAA), which became a sort of militant political caucus for homosexuals in a number of cities.

In New York, as in other cities, the GAA and related organizations began to lobby vigorously for the end of discrimination against homosexuals in housing and employment. The proposed legislation touched off sensitive psychic fears embedded deep in the American culture. Still, new literature and medical observations, arguing that traditional sex and family roles should be reconsidered and that homosexuality should no longer be regarded as an illness, found a great deal of attention nationally.

In some cities, the Gays made legislative gains. But, in New York City, the Gays tried year after year to pass a nondiscrimination bill in the city council without success. Some militants began to take out their frustrations by helping to defeat John Lindsay, then mayor of New York. At a movie opening intended to raise money for Lindsay's presidential campaign in early 1972, Gay Activist hecklers disrupted Lindsay's address, forcing him to retreat to the wings. The emotions seething through the GAA movement were as heated as those in other political crusades.

Yet in the early 1970s, the GAA members were gradually gaining political acumen and tactical shrewdness. By the first months of 1972, the GAA and a number of other homosexual groups were sufficiently organized and strong to meet in Chicago to form the National Coalition of Gay Organizations and to adopt a political platform of Gay rights. The intention of the coalition was to proselytize for a sexual rights plank in the platform of each major party.

I was present at the first Democratic platform hearing in Faneuil Hall in Boston, in May 1972. The Gays were superbly organized as participants — better prepared, indeed, than some of the local women's caucuses. At the doorway, several men stood handing out kits on homosexual rights to reporters and other visitors. Included in the parcels was a slickly produced booklet entitled *Twenty Questions About Homosexuality, a Political Primer,* published by the GAA, arguing that homosexuals "are neither criminal, immoral nor sick." There were also reprints of letters from George McGovern and Hubert Humphrey endorsing the aims of the GAA. The Humphrey letter stated: "I see no reason why homosexual Americans should be excluded from equal protection under the law . . . Homosexuals are citizens; let us treat them as such . . ."

Inside the ancient hall, Ernest O. Reaugh of the National Coalition of Gay Organizations testified:

> There are today more than 500 gay liberation groups actively working in the United States. Others are starting at such a rapid rate it has led Professor Laud Humphreys, sociologist at the State University of New York, to declare the gay liberation movement to be the fastest growing social movement in the country today. These groups represent over 50,000 openly avowed homosexual women and men.
>
> But these are only the visible tip of a giant iceberg. The gay subculture is of mammoth proportions. The late Dr. Kinsey told us in the 1940's when he published that 10% of all adult males and nearly as many females have primarily homosexual relationships. This is 1 in 10 of all people and it means there are today 15–20,000,000 homosexual citizens in the United States — after women, the largest minority in this country.[16]

The Minorities Rise Up

If the Kinsey figure was to be believed, the potential political power of the Gay movement clearly was colossal. However, Reaugh did not address himself to what really mattered — that is, the effectiveness of leadership and discipline within the Gay organizations, which was still weak. Nor did Reaugh mention the internal ideological conflicts with transvestites and lesbians among the almost exclusively male Gays. And he neglected to report on the disinclination of many brethren to confess publicly their sexual orientation. These factors reduced the chances that Gays would quickly accomplish their goals in the seventies.

Nonetheless, the new National Coalition had some success at Democratic state conventions. In April 1972, both the New York NDC and the New York State Democratic Committee adopted almost word for word a plank on sexual discrimination proposed originally by the National Coalition. It read:

Millions of Gay women and men in this country are subject to severe social, economic, psychological and legal oppression because of their sexual orientation. We affirm the right of all persons to define and express their own sensibility, emotionality and sexuality, and to choose their own life styles, so long as they do not infringe upon the rights of others. We pledge an end to all social, economic and legal oppression of Gay women and men. We urge the repeal of all laws forbidding and interfering with voluntary sex acts between consenting adults in private.

A few days later, the preprimary state Democratic convention in Oregon passed a plank saying: "We commit the Democratic Party to use the full force of its powers to achieve equal rights for all homosexually-oriented individuals." In Des Moines, Iowa, the following month, where McGovern supporters controlled the state convention, the Iowa party ap-

187

proved a plank stating: "Laws dealing with sexual activities between consenting adults should be repealed." This lobbying by the Gays at the various state conventions soon paid off in homosexual delegates and alternates, mainly from New York, to the Democratic Convention in Miami. By July, pressure was rising on the convention to adopt a prohomosexuality plank. We on the platform staff were well aware of the growing sentiment among many groups for some sort of reference in the platform to sexual freedom. Women favored any language recognizing people's sexual independence, since it would, in effect, permit legal abortions.

All of this was cause for great and natural distress to McGovern. He was fearful that Nixon would use abortion and homosexuality in the fall campaign as Humphrey and Jackson had used the three A's — acid, abortion, amnesty — against him in the Nebraska primary, and thereby distract voters from the deeper issues. So he sent down the order to the platform staff to fight any language on sexuality in the Democratic platform that he had not himself approved.

Yet it was impossible to exclude the Gay forces from the discussions at Miami. Theodore White perceptively described the trap into which McGovern had put himself:

> What was moving across camera was a family discussion within the dominant left wing concerning the platform, program, and purpose to which it would bend the old Democratic Party. On most major matters, McGovern control could hold firm . . . But by the very philosophy of "participatory democracy" that had recruited its marchers, it could not impose discipline without first allowing debate . . . [thus] came homosexuals to the microphone and camera, men openly demanding before the nation that the coupling of males be accepted not furtively, but as a natural and legal right.[17]

As this debate ensued, the McGovern platform staff was instructed to produce a supporter who would speak against the Gays. A woman delegate volunteered. I happened by chance to see the text of the address that the Democratic National Committee staff (not the McGovern operation) had given to her. It was crassly antihomosexual, almost designed to provoke the Gays in the auditorium into outraged protest. When the woman finished, the convention's galleries, crammed with Gay activists, exploded in jeers and catcalls. All of this sizzled over national television. Still, in the end, after all the exertion and noise on both sides, the Gay rights plank failed to pass.

Thereafter, homosexuality died as a continuing controversy in the campaign, despite (as the Watergate hearing showed) Republican attempts to keep it alive by sending people purporting to be homosexual to wave banners at McGovern rallies. Later, commentators and politicians tried to fix the blame for McGovern's defeat on, among other things, the Gay protesters at Miami. They argued that the Miami convention — with its potpourri of blacks, Chicanos, Gays, militant women — disgusted the middle-class citizens of the country and indelibly stained McGovern as a "far-out radical."

This seemed to me a forced conclusion. As I noted earlier, Nixon's accomplishment in 1972 was to put together the 13.5 percent of the vote polled by Wallace in 1968 with his own 43.4 percent, to which his manipulation of the racial issue added a fraction of the normally Democratic low-income white vote in the North. No Democratic candidate committed to civil rights could have done much better than McGovern. If Humphrey might have held more of the white working class, McGovern probably did better among the young. Furthermore, it was difficult to see how McGovern —

or any other Democratic candidate — could control the Gays. They had their rights as delegates to raise issues and demonstrate. McGovern, in particular, would have compromised all his self-proclaimed principles of "letting a thousand flowers bloom" had he insisted on shutting off the debate.

After the 1972 election, the Gay movement seemed to crumble. Gay activist Arthur Bell wrote in *The Village Voice* a year and a half later: "Is the Gay Activists Alliance dead? Did it die along with SDS, the Fugs, the draft lottery, tie-dyed-T-shirts, love beads, street people, and Intro 475 [the bill to outlaw discrimination against homosexuals in housing and employment]? Or is it valiantly struggling, reaching out for help, groping to keep its head above water, and will it survive?" The prognosis was poor, said Bell. A year and a half of in-fighting had gradually turned the New York GAA from a caucus of idealists into a bevy of political factions, and its membership had dwindled.[18]

Finagling took place. Committee chairmanships were "bought." It was just like what was happening politically on the outside. Disenchantment crept in. The manipulativeness that had been playing bingo in our unliberated lives was playing tic tac toe with our lives in the movement. Minorities within minorities caught on. Is there a place for us at GAA, asked the transvestites. What about us, asked the women. Ultimately, the answer was no place. The organization was primarily white middle-class male.[19]

Sexism infiltrated even the Gay movement.

Yet, Bell pointed out, there was one success story — a new offshoot of the GAA, the National Gay Task Force. This organization held a fund-raising party in Manhattan in 1974 and managed to attract a number of well-known liberal

politicians, among them Allard Lowenstein, the former Demo-
cratic congressman and former chairman of ADA; Elinor
Guggenheimer, the head of New York City's Consumer
Affairs office; and one New York City councilman. The
Bronx borough president, while not present, was a public
advocate of the GAA's goals.

Indeed, by mid-1974, at least ten cities, including Min-
neapolis and Washington, had enacted variations of homosexual rights laws by amending municipal codes or passing
comprehensive civil rights packages. According to a *New York
Times* report, the laws were less significant to the Gays than
the political organizations that homosexuals formed to promote them. "Strategists among the homosexual leadership
speak of the laws as tools rather than as ends in themselves.
They view the laws — and the publicity campaigns that help
them pass — as consciousness-raising vehicles, for the community at large and for homosexuals 'who need that security
to help them come out of the closet,' as one of the leaders of
the political effort said."[20]

In the seventies, then, these four minorities emerged as
genuine interest groups in reform politics. They established
organizations, participated in campaigns, undertook fund-raising, ran their own candidates. Where there were enough of
them, they acted as influential voting blocs. Liberal candidates began to seek their backing.

Now, in the mid-seventies, the public's cautious, sometimes
hostile, attitude toward them seems to be shifting. Where
once the groups used to upset voters deeply, the public today
mainly distrusts the government. Minorities are generally regarded as the victims of unfair harassment. Polls taken by

Louis Harris in 1973 and 1974 show Americans increasingly sympathetic to the disenfranchised.

The Puerto Ricans and the Chicanos continue to have substantial and growing political power because they have organized voters in key states. Disorganization and lack of effective leadership still blight the causes of the Indians and the Gays. But liberal politicians are realists in their search for sympathetic constituents. They are not likely to disregard any of these four rising minorities as they look for winning coalitions.

8 ☆

The Spirit of '76

THE EMERGENCE of nonparty movements working inside and outside both major parties fits into the pattern that political scientists like Walter Dean Burnham have described in recent years as "politics without parties." Independent ideological movements have risen to fill the vacuum left as both the Democratic and Republican parties shrink in their command of the electorate. In 1974, for example, only 21 percent of voters identified themselves as Republicans, 48 percent identified themselves as Democrats, 26 percent said they were independents.[1] Increasing numbers of voters seemed to believe that their interests are better represented in the new movements than in the old politics.

Yet the new groups are frail craft in the turbulent seas of United States politics. Many are organizations, as the preceding chapters suggest, both new and untried. Most have short histories — some springing out of the 1968 campaign, others rising from the presidential politics of 1972. Fresh ones are likely to appear by 1976.

The movements have existed at both ends of the political spectrum. No doubt the largest single movement is that inchoately gathered behind the personality of George Wallace. But there are more groups on the left than on the right, and, while the reform movements vary among themselves in size and impact, the ingredients may now exist for the makings of a reform coalition capable of capturing a national majority. For the political realities of the seventies are accelerating the growth of the reform movements today — the weakness of the parties, the changes within them, the zeal of the movements outside parties, the ability of reformers to raise money for causes, the emergence of fresh issues to link together low-income whites and minorities, the failures of conservative policies, and the advent of dozens of new reformers.

While these new constituencies have fostered independent reform power centers that straddle party lines, they have also evolved secure coalitions within each party. The enactment of proportional representation and affirmative-action reforms by the Democrats, first of all, has entirely reshaped their national convention (including their 1974 mid-term convention), and their state organizations, to the advantage of the new movements; the voluntary reforms for the selection of delegates promulgated by the Republicans have placed at least a moral obligation on the forthcoming Republican National Convention and the state Rule 29 Commissions to initiate action on minorities.

There is, in addition, a further development strengthening reform politics within the parties — the extraordinary ability of the new reformers, backed by their cadres, to raise large sums of money for the support of specific goals, as in the presidential elections of 1968 and 1972. In 1968, antiwar sentiment enabled the two reformist Democratic senators, Robert Kennedy and Eugene McCarthy, to raise collectively in the primaries some $20 million, twice as much as was contributed to their prowar adversaries, President Johnson and Vice-President Humphrey.[2] Two Republicans, Governor Nelson Rockefeller and Governor George Romney, thought of as being opposed to escalation, raised almost $10 million for their primary races against Richard Nixon (who himself spent about $10 million and kept his solution to the war a secret), although they drew mainly on wealthy friends and family sources, rather than on small contributors.[3] Senator George McGovern, when he campaigned for the 1972 nomination and then ran for the presidency, raised over $38 million on Vietnam and the reform issues, over half the amount coming from small donors.[4]

The first inkling of this ability of the progressives to raise funds came in the 1968 primaries. The campaigns of Senators McCarthy and Kennedy conclusively proved that issue-oriented candidacies could survive financially. Both men, running against an incumbent president in their own party, had, out of necessity, to base their campaigns on guerrilla movements called into action by antiwar feelings. While Kennedy, for the most part, depended for his money on either family sources or wealthy admirers, McCarthy, starting the race five months earlier, enlisted the aid of fifty large donors — and then compiled a roll of about 150,000 small contributors, using lists provided by various antiwar coalitions and liberal organizations, and employing direct mail and advertising techniques pioneered by Senator Barry Goldwater in his grass-roots uprising in the Republican Party in 1964.[5]

Then, in 1972, the McGovern workers transformed McCarthy's pocket-change technology into a large-scale, sophisticated, computerized operation. McGovern, of course, was not a legendary and a glamorous candidate like Robert Kennedy, so he could not depend on personality alone to attract supporters and donors; nor was he the instantaneous hero Eugene McCarthy became after the New Hampshire primary. Rather, McGovern's battle was waged with slow tactical maneuvers and was virtually unpublicized; it was dependent mainly on his own gallant purpose and on a band of irregulars foraging for food and supplies off the countryside. McGovern's success, it seems, was to perceive that issues related directly to fund-raising and organization. McGovern took note of the profound emotions roused in the liberal electorate by the war, which he, as an antiwar candidate, could tap. As a reformer, he also reached out to constituencies who felt abandoned by both political parties. His crucial decision was to use mail drives to locate and stimulate these people — rather than television (for which he had no money) — a strategy he had used successfully in his South Dakota senatorial campaigns.

For years, McGovern had collected lists of sympathizers. Jeff Smith, one of his closest aides and a former Robert Kennedy organizer in South Dakota, accompanied him on his travels after the 1968 convention, recording the names and addresses of McGovern's acquaintances for the three-by-five card file in McGovern's office. Smith subsequently explained: "McGovern had a unique way of getting names for his list. He might stop in a bar in Albuquerque, New Mexico, and inquire of a person who seemed friendly to his views, 'Say, where are you from?' Then he would ask for the person's address . . . I don't know if anybody was aware of what we were doing."[6]

McGovern himself was also deeply involved in the peace movement. In May 1970, he helped sponsor a television program opposing the Cambodian invasion, in which he and Harold Hughes, and two Republicans, Senators Mark Hatfield and Charles Goodell, appeared as speakers. Some $70,000 were spent to buy thirty minutes of prime-time television, and an appeal at the end of the program brought in almost $500,000 from 50,000 viewers. The response was symptomatic of the deep feelings of the electorate on the war issue. When the time came for his own declaration, McGovern used the names (though it was unclear who actually owned the lists). He also accumulated other lists from "peace" activities. He had access to a large pool of contributors gathered by the venerable antiwar organization, SANE. In 1970, he signed a letter to raise money for the 1970 Campaign Fund, an independent group set up to provide support for five senators who were antiwar liberals, and he retained that list.

McGovern decided to declare thirteen months before the first primary, largely to counter his weakness in the polls (between 2 percent and 3 percent) and to beat a path to the doors of the ideological donors and reform activists before anyone else did. To increase public recognition, McGovern worked out a plan to use his lists for sending a letter of announcement to his friends and to the nation's newspaper editors, following the example of candidates in the first years of the Republic. I remember, when I was in New York, receiving a bulging envelope containing the McGovern letter, and feeling quite stirred by the drama of the written announcement. Though hardly an unbiased recipient, I was impressed by McGovern's courage in declaring and asking for contributions at such an early date in the presidential race, an action which was quixotic, but electrifying. Other people were similarly affected, for the results were extraordinary. The letter raised $330,000 from

16,000 contributors, a truly phenomenal 7 percent return. "In January 1971," as Frank Mankiewicz, the campaign director, later explained, "the situation was ripe for a war protest candidate. On Vietnam Humphrey was Johnson, Muskie was Humphrey. Nixon hadn't ended the war. Labor was controlled by hawks. There was a sellout to Muskie's vague antiwar position by Democratic governors like Gilligan and Shapp. Out of this poured a lot of protest money."[7]

McGovern sent follow-up mailings to the 16,000 men and women who had responded to his first appeal to ask them to become members of the President's Club. Over 10 percent joined. By the end of 1971, the number had risen from 1800 to 7000. By the primaries, 9000 were enrolled.[8] Indeed, these mailings were McGovern's most important fund-raising enterprises. An average of $70,000 to $80,000 poured into campaign headquarters every thirty days, paying for office rent, limited field operations, and salaries. As the head of the research and issues staff of the McGovern campaign, Ted van Dyk, reflected in *The Washington Monthly*:

> It is forgotten now, but back in mid and late 1971, Harold Hughes, Birch Bayh, Fred Harris, William Proxmire, John Lindsay, and Shirley Chisholm (not to mention Edmund Muskie or Hubert Humphrey) were running ahead, close behind, or even with George McGovern in the national political polls. The difference was that they didn't have the mailing list and the money it brought in. One by one they dropped out, leaving only Lindsay and Chisholm to compete with McGovern as the "serious candidates" in the primaries.[9]

Once the liberal competitors faded and McGovern beat Hubert Humphrey in California, McGovern emerged as the only solvent Democratic candidate.

The preconvention period ended with 100,000 donors and about $5 million. After his nomination, McGovern set up the Million Member Club, and raised almost six times as much money as he had in the preconvention period. Again using massive mail drives and television pitches, utilizing Vietnam and Watergate, McGovern drew forth a huge outpouring of contributions in August, September, and October, despite a floundering campaign, rejection by the AFL-CIO and many party regulars, and the Eagleton mess.

The signal lesson of the McGovern funding effort was that it amply demonstrated the effectiveness of mailings — and of television appeals — that stressed deeply-felt reform issues. Nearly 700,000 small contributors donated about 65 percent of the $38 million he raised — a total that, incidentally, was higher than any previous Democratic candidate ever raised and that left his campaign free of debt. McGovern opened up a new, very promising source of revenue for his party. Many of the small donations were from professionals — doctors, lawyers, academicians, entertainers, and other self-employed persons. As one political scientist from the Ripon Society commented: ". . . this enormous display of support among the professional class constitutes a milestone in political fund-raising because it broadens dramatically the sociological base of democratic finance."[10]

But, ironically, this new financial surge for reformers arrived at a most awkward time in history. After the election, Congress began to tighten up on the campaign spending laws as a consequence of the Watergate scandals. Yet one of the authors of a Ripon Society study of the 1972 contributors to the presidential campaigns, *The Jaws of Victory*, argued quite convincingly in the *Wall Street Journal* that, rather than hurting the reformers' cash flow, the new "campaign reform proposals will tend to help the more ideological or cause-oriented candidate at the expense of the more traditional middle-of-the-road aspirant. Just as the new rules of delegate selection in the Democratic Party helped George Wallace and George McGovern, so will the new finance rules help the same kinds of candidates in the future."[11] Why? Because though Congress has placed a low limit on individual contributions, issue-oriented candidates can still harvest their cash crop from hundreds of small donors. And though Congress has set a ceiling on overall spending by individual candidates, reformers can make up for the limit in total funds by drawing on the armies of unpaid volunteers provided by the reform groups.

Public financing, too, will still help all candidates, in particular reformers like McGovern and conservatives. For example, the existence of the tax check-off system (which allows any person who pays income taxes to designate one dollar of his payments for transfer to a general fund for the presidential election and, under certain stringent conditions, to the primaries), has shifted all fund-raising to the primary period alone, thereby reducing a reform candidate's cash outlay for a long campaign and allowing the candidate to focus attention on those issues that stimulate emotional giving.

However, McGovern's dismal showing in 1972 demonstrated clearly that there were grave dangers associated with building reform coalitions, raising money, and collecting votes on emotional issues alone — even if it was the only way to win the nomination in a multicandidate primary system. For a candidate's issues might, like those of McGovern, appeal only to a small segment of the populace and frighten off the remainder.

In a study conducted by the University of Michigan Center for Political Studies shortly after the 1972 election, four political scientists nonetheless concluded that McGovern was correct to focus deliberately on issues.[12] The 1972 electorate, they said, was more inclined to make ideological instead of party-based or personality judgments on candidates than in any previous contemporary election — but, they added, the majority was not yet ready to accept McGovern's ideas. Notwithstanding his loss, they noted: "It may be argued . . . that since McGovern's supporters formed 58 percent of the Democrats, that rather than an elite, they are the vanguard of a liberalizing trend occurring not only in the ranks of the Democrats but in the population as a whole. Thus, McGovern's principal error may have been in overestimating the speed of the population trend."[13]

The introduction of ideology, the researchers asserted, is, in fact, reconstituting the make-up of the two political parties in profound ways that cannot be clearly foreseen. It may be leading to the realignment of the parties along conservative-liberal lines. It may even be eroding the basis of the two-party system itself. Ideology is, in short, a tremendous catalyst for change.

As proof of this contention, the Michigan study pointed to the ideological split within the Democratic Party. There were now greater differences, they said, between the two Democratic factions — the Humphrey fans and Wallace followers in 1968, the McGovern crusaders and the Democrats for Nixon in 1972 — than there were between Democrats and Republicans. "Even with respect to the liberal-conservative measure, the differences between Democrats and Republicans were less extreme than those between the two Democratic factions."[14] This finding essentially confirmed the original perception of reformers that in the Democratic Party, and perhaps in the Republican Party, there was no tenable "center" position. Control of the party really depended on which ideological faction could win enough delegates through the primaries to seize the party's nomination, not on one candidate's being more "centrist" than another.

One of the reasons this was happening, the Michigan study adduced, was that the electorate was significantly changing in its composition, becoming a professional and educated electorate — the sort of constituency on which McGovern drew heavily for his small donors in 1972. The Michigan statistics showed that voter turnout rates among the college-educated increased from 26 percent in 1964 to 37 percent in 1972, while the turnout among those not so well educated declined in that period. And the college-educated, the Michigan political scientists reported, find it "apparently far easier . . . to directly translate issue attitudes into a vote decision than for the relatively less well-educated."[15]

Louis Harris in his book, *The Anguish of Change*, confirmed the trend toward an increasingly more educated electorate. His polling in the early seventies led him to project for 1976 an electorate with a marked increase in voters who are college-educated, who receive incomes of $15,000 and over, who are political independents, who live in suburbia, who are under thirty, and who have professional occupations. He predicted for 1976 a concomitant decline in the number of voters who have under $10,000 per year income, who live in small towns, who are union members, whose education did not advance beyond the eighth grade, who are registered Democrats and Republicans. He concluded that in 1976 there will be "a pluralistic, highly selective American electorate. It would quickly turn aside the easy rhetoric of politicians who promised them easy panaceas. By any previous standards in the history of the world, it would be an elitist country in quality, but for the first time it would be on a mass basis. More important, these voters would be a society capable of thinking in large terms about the world and about the quality of life around them at home."[16]

To this highly affective electorate, it would seem that a candidate who rides with the reformers would probably have a greater appeal than one who hides from them — for the purpose of collecting votes as well as money. Thus, McGovern's fundamental weakness, besides his obvious difficulties with the Eagleton affair, may have been his inability, in 1972, to present the issues clearly to a national constituency — not his having raised the issues in the first place.

Since the 1972 election, however, reformers themselves have split on how best to formulate and articulate issues for 1976. For the most part, they embrace the ideas generated by the new young workers, but they show deep perplexity on the problem of proceeding from that foundation to reach the constituencies they lost in 1972 — the blue-collar workers, the ethnic groups, the party regulars, and the Wallace followers. This bewilderment affects the powerful reformers in the Democratic Party; it also raises questions about the future success of the smaller faction in the Republican Party.

The actual issues have not changed. Reformers are dealing with the same domestic issues they have dealt with for decades — tax reform, unequal distribution of wealth, corporate control, guaranteed minimum income, civil rights, full employment, inflation, reduction in defense spending, elimination of poverty, a national health care system. The question, rather, is how to present these issues to both a professional, educated electorate and to a blue-collar constituency.

It is a conundrum that goes back to the very essence of the reformers' philosophy. The reformers have talked about greater equality in the distribution of income, yet have not effectively brought home to the American people the failure of the society, in the years since the New Deal and World War II, to alter the patterns by which income is distributed. One small example: the bottom 20 percent of all American families earned 5.1 percent of the national income in 1947; twenty-five years later, in 1972, they earned 5.4 percent. The wealthiest 5 percent collected 17.5 percent of income in 1947; in 1972 they took 15.9 percent of the national income.[17]

The reformers have also not successfully roused the nation to the accelerating, ever-increasing power of the country's largest corporations — power that has grown despite trust-busting, regulatory agencies, and congressional oversight. They have not stirred the voters' wrath over the most outrageous abuses of the so-called "free enterprise system." One example: the Washington *Post* in 1973, quoting from a Senate study of the thirty principal holders of voting stock in corporations, reported that eight institutions, including six banks, controlled or dominated most of the country's largest corporations.[18] In addition, a 1974 Congressional study revealed that ten major corporations with income totaling nearly $1 billion legally paid no federal tax at all in 1973.[19]

The reformers now have several matters to work with in the seventies, which may make presentation of their basic economic plans for a redistributive program easier. It is clear that there remains a reservoir of populist, reformist spirit in the electorate. Thus, in the year of Nixon's landslide, the American voters elected a heavily liberal Senate and House. Also, the reform cadres have survived, and nonpartisan organizations, like public-interest law firms, Nader-type operations, and Common Cause have prospered. "Stagflation," the "energy crisis," and Watergate have stirred the people against the large, impersonal institutions of corporations and government.

Indeed, the dissatisfaction is now so widespread it is a two-party phenomenon. As Alice M. Rivlin, former Assistant Secretary of Health, Education, and Welfare, and a member of the Brookings Institution, wrote in 1973:

> It is fashionable among the doomsayers these days to put the blame for lack of social progress on deep divisions in the country over social objectives and what ought to be done to reach them. Actually, though, agreement on desirable directions of social change seems remarkably wide. Three themes recur in the platforms and political oratory of both major parties: (1) opportunities, incomes, and access to essential services ought to be more equal than they are; (2) public services for everyone ought to be more effective than they are; (3) the Federal government ought to be doing something about both these problems.[20]

But reformers have some things working against them, especially racism. Samuel Lubell made the perceptive point, in *The Hidden Crisis in American Politics*, that "In all elections to come, until our racial conflict is resolved, a sizeable segment of the voters will be turned between racial antipathies and the economic pull of the Democratic Party. Which of these emotions wrestles to the top will shift from election to election, as racial tensions ease or intensify, as economic satisfactions fall or rise."[21]

These political realities suggest that for a reform candidate to overcome racial antipathies and to propound economic change successfully he must behave like a Robert Kennedy. He must persuade low-income whites and poor minorities that their economic interests are the same. A black man, Vernon Jordan, President of the Urban League, placed this central truth in a unique perspective in 1973, when he described the common economic crunch faced by whites and blacks over welfare, housing, manpower training, and employment:

> There are three times as many poor white families as there are poor black families. The majority of people on welfare are white. Of the black poor, over half don't get one single devalued dollar from welfare. Two-thirds of the families who got homes through [a major] housing subsidy program were white. Two-thirds of the trainees in [manpower] programs are white; three-fourths of on-the-job training enrollees are white, and four-fifths of the people employed in the public employment are white . . . [black Americans] must demonstrate to white Americans that our cause is, in effect, their own, and we must be willing to cross racial lines to build the coalitions around issues of importance to both blacks and whites.[22]

In the search for methods to present the economic issues and to quiet racial fears, several different approaches have developed in the early seventies among the reformers. One of the most far-reaching and radical has been advanced by Harvard economist John Kenneth Galbraith in *Economics and the Public Purpose*.[23] He has propounded a form of American socialism that, he believes, will retake control of the economy from the great United States corporations and give it back to the people.

Galbraith argues that an oligopolic planning system now dominates the country, indirectly controlling what is left of the free market system. It skewers social and economic development, enforces inequality, and befouls foreign policy. The government must regain control, contends Galbraith, not by breaking up corporations through classical antitrust action, but by nationalizing "mature" corporations that have achieved near-total independence of the market; by establishing public ownership in areas like housing and transportation, where the private sector is inefficient and atomized; and by granting assistance for smaller enterprises in the market sector — small retailers, repairmen, domestics, auto body shops, and so on. For the small businessmen, Galbraith would suspend the antitrust laws so that they might join together, mobilize their power, and fix their price structures, as the large corporations do. Finally, Galbraith would provide a decent annual income to the poorest in society, and strengthen the progressive tax system.

The Galbraith approach touches on the basic economic issues that have absorbed reformers in the last decade: tax reform, corporate control, guaranteed minimun income, full employment, slicing defense spending, unequal distribution of wealth. His program in some ways, indeed, resembles the old McGovern platform of 1972. His solutions, however, are far more drastic.

The experiences of the 1968 and 1972 elections, and of Richard Nixon's abruptly terminated tenure, though, have scarred once innocent political sensibilities. In two principal areas Galbraith's proposals arouse apprehension. First: is it possible for a reform candidate to create a political coalition around Galbraith's radical measures without resurrecting the fear that the reforms will be used to transfer money from the white blue-collar worker to the nonwhite (a fear that arose over the McGovern $1000-a-year minimum income plan);

207

second, is it possible to control a future Nixon if the government he commands has increased power over the economy and uses it to corrupt or plunder the political opposition? Galbraith's answer to both fears is that the undercurrents of economic history and of the "public cognizance" (recognition by the public of its own best interests) and, finally, of a strengthened Congress — "the natural voice of the public purpose" — will prevail.

Galbraith may be placing inordinate faith in indefinite movements, the "public cognizance," and troubled governmental institutions — none of which has done especially well in our contemporary history. It seems as appropriate to consider another economic approach suggested by reformers — the diffusion of power by antitrust actions and by decentralization of authority. To diffuse power would not remove it from the hands of public citizens; the power would simply be parceled out to smaller units of local interest, thereby creating a mixed level of authority. There are evident difficulties with such decentralization — the question of who should receive the powers at local levels, the question of how to control the spending of resources, the issues of efficiency and bureaucracy. But a tilting of governmental powers toward many levels of society — particularly to those people most hurt by the decisions of invisible administrators — does impart the hope that people in all parts of the country can regain an ancient spirit of community.

Nonetheless, Galbraith's notion of socialism is now a lively topic among reformers, who recognize that it can no longer be easily put off to some vague future. Many Democratic intellectuals have declared an interest. For example, Michael Harrington, author of *The Other America*, in 1973 formed a socialist group, called the Democratic Socialist Organizing

Committee, within the Democratic Party. He suggested in an interview that same year that the Democratic Party is open to socialist ideas: "We must go where the people are, which is the liberal wing of the Democratic Party." Indeed, he said, "If you take away the word socialism, you could very easily propose a program in the Democratic Party which would be acceptable to Socialists."[24] The founding platform of the DSOC itself stated: "We support, of course, the immediate reforms advocated by the progressive forces of the labor and liberal movements: a right to a job for every able-bodied citizen . . . tax justice . . . a guaranteed annual income . . . But our socialist convictions cause us to champion these increments of change in a distinctive way, so as to make them attack the very structure of injustice."[25]

Clearly, then, the reformers' solutions have now converged with parts of a Democratic socialist program and vice versa, but whether the reformers ultimately embrace nationalization, or decentralization, or a mixture of both, their search is for *wholesale* redistributive changes for the country. But the success of any scheme rests on what, I believe, Galbraith himself was hinting at in his notion of "public cognizance" — some sort of enlightened reformist leadership to articulate the profound anxieties of the American people and, on that basis, to win elections and begin the structural changes that reformers have been urging on America for the past decade.

In other words, the reform groups cannot do the job themselves. As women, as blacks, labor unions, legislators, middle-class liberals, and ethnic minorities, they can create and sustain the atmosphere that makes people attentive to reform ideas. They can stir the emotions of the political activists. But, as Joseph Rauh, Jr., once remarked, "We have always been a minority. We made the mistake in nineteen seventy-two of thinking we were a majority. We are really a minority in search of a coalition. We win when we persuade the middle. We win by using issues to woo the center, as, for example, the election of 1932 when Franklin Roosevelt persuaded the middle to cast their ballots for the Democrats because the nation was hungry."[26]

The search for an FDR-type leadership to stir the middle and the left is the search for a reformer who can reconcile factions. This is a continuing theme in American political life. The man or woman who, in E. M. Forster's words, can "only connect" with all the people, who can identify with their needs or demonstrate a capacity to feel and care about their lives, is the person who may have the influence to move them in the direction of fundamental social change.

Of the two parties, the possibility of a reformist leadership in the Republican Party is today paradoxically the weakest and the strongest. It is the weakest because the party is still tightly tied to the big corporations of the country for its financial support; it is still beholden to narrow laissez-faire values; it is a minority party that has lost voters every year for a decade, to the point where there are now 5 percent fewer Republicans than independents; its reform wing is lame; and it is damaged by massive mistakes in dealing with the economy and by the worst political scandal in American history.

Yet the horrors of the Nixon years are likely to force many Republican administrations for years to come to stay clean. The party is like Al Capp's Joe Btfsplk — fated to have a malevolent storm cloud constantly hanging over its head, which threatens to detonate at the slightest whiff of scandal or favoritism.

In this atmosphere, any Republican — President Ford,

Nelson Rockefeller, Ronald Reagan — will pay homage to the reformist forces within the party. And should Ford, for any reason, leave office in 1976, a reformist Republican may be the logical successor, because of the widespread discontent among party moderates and some "conscience" conservatives over the political disarray in the Republican Party. These people will be looking for a leader who, in the tradition of Theodore Roosevelt or Wendell Willkie, will break the hammerlock of Republican conservatism and seek an independent course.

If such a candidate does arise, the changed party rules may produce the necessary allies for the cause. The rules strongly favor the representation of women — a growing progressive bloc in the party — who may make up 50 percent of the delegations to the 1976 convention. The new party rules also call for representation of "young people, minority and heritage groups and senior citizens . . ." These phrases are still undefined, and compliance with the rules is, in any event, voluntary, but a well-organized campaign may be able to draw on large numbers of youth and minority groups under the aegis of the rules. A candidate may, for instance, be able to persuade some of the other reform-minded voters, like the blacks and the members of progressive labor unions, to become involved in the battle for the Republican Party.

Such a nomination is still a long shot because reform views continue to grate on many party faithful and because regulars distrust candidates with independent views. But in an age of disillusionment in government, integrity is the by-word, and, in the swiftly changing electorate and in a moment of weak parties, the reformer may yet be able to piece together the right moderate coalition, which could eventually take over the Republican Party.

A reformer is in a much stronger position in the Democratic Party. The new reformers no longer exercise a negative veto on the next Democratic nominee. They are now the final arbiters in his or her selection. The left is, in the 1970s, the most potent political broker. As Tom Wicker has observed:

> Senator McGovern's nomination in 1972 was to a great extent due to divided and inept opposition, but it still demonstrated (a) that a lot of Democrats would support a candidate on the left, (b) that there was plenty of organizational and other political talent among the "kids," the "reformers," and the "radicals," and (c) that the left could raise both big and little money to finance a major campaign. All those things are still true and will be in 1976, particularly since women and minority groups and young people, many of them finding their homes on the Democratic left, have come so heavily into party politics. It seems fair to estimate that, even without a unifying personality or issue, the kind of forces that nominated McGovern in 1972 make up at least a third of the Democratic Party and are potentially even stronger. Given the new delegate selection procedures, which do away with the unit rule at every level and guarantee delegate strength proportional to voting strength for each primary candidate, the left therefore ought to be able to field a formidable candidate at the 1976 convention.[27]

But the reform organizations — and their candidates — still face severe trials in the coming years. The handicaps of building a well-constructed coalition remain immense — the uncertainty over the impact of the delegate reforms in both parties, particularly the role of the state affirmative-action programs; the self-righteousness and exclusivism of some reformers; the chronic inability of many cadres to forge permanent majority coalitions; the difficulty in deciding which issues are important and how to present them; the hostility of many low-income whites to nonwhite minorities (and vice versa); the role of Gerald Ford's incumbency; and the lack of knowledge about the quality of the reform leadership that will rise up in both parties to organize and lead the coalitions. Any of these may produce calamities that could wreck the formation of a reformist majority.

One further though largely unspoken theme weaves its way into the political calculations of the 1970s — that is the role of fear: the dread of crime and violence, the alarm that demands "law and order" at any price, the corrosive anxiety that manifests itself in ill-will toward minorities, the irrational fright that makes people turn to demagogues or religious fanatics for solace. This is a profound emotional terror, which the reformers of the seventies can no longer pretend does not exist. As J. W. Anderson wrote in the Washington *Post,* "One moral of the political year 1972 seems to be that fear corrodes political standards. It is a familiar truth. People do not like being frightened and they are willing to tolerate a great deal — rumors of scandal, abrasions of civil liberties, erosions of constitutions — if they consider it to be the price of some measure of stability in their private lives."[28]

The reform coalitions of the later seventies, whatever their platforms may be, must be willing to present their ideas within the traditions of the Republic or face a grave loss of trust by the voters. The reformers cannot simply disregard the existence of a "silent majority." Instead, they must reach out to the anxieties of people whose lives are perched precariously on the edges of poverty, and reassure them that change does not mean loss of self-esteem or wealth, or mugging in the streets. It is in this dangerous area where the reformers may trip and set off the psychic grenades they planted in 1972.

The reformers, however, have the currents of history flowing with them. Their movements have penetrated deeply into American society and they have survived public scrutiny. Television has made them familiar to millions of Americans and has raised the consciousness of the electorate. In the immediate future, the movements rather than the parties are going to be the vital outlets for the political energies of American society. Given the right circumstances, it is no longer inconceivable that the new reformers could produce a candidate and a political constituency that could control the federal government by 1976. The improbable may now be the possible.

NOTES & INDEX

Notes

CHAPTER 1

1. See Alan Baron, *Democratic Planning Group Newsletter*, March 1, 1973 for fuller details.
2. "The Commission on Party Structure and Delegate Selection to the Democratic National Committee," Report of the Commission, *Mandate for Reform* (Washington, D.C., April 1970), p. 34.
3. "The Commission on Party Structure and Delegate Selection to the Democratic National Committee," Final Report of the Commission, *The Party Reformed* (Washington, D.C., July, 1972), p. 8.
4. Jack Newfield, "Of Reform, Hacks, and Guideline Junkies," *The Village Voice*, July 20, 1972.
5. "The Commission on Delegate Selection and Party Structure to the Democratic National Committee," Final Report of the Commission, *Democrats All* (Washington, D.C., December 1973), p. 21.
6. Christopher Lyden, "Democratic Reforms: Using Rules to Make Ends Meet," *New York Times*, November 4, 1973.
7. Interview with Representative William Steiger (Wisconsin), Washington, D.C., January 25, 1974.
8. Interview with Bobbie Greene Kilberg, Washington, D.C., January 18, 1974.
9. Dr. Ronald Walters, "Democratic Party Guidelines: Full Role for Blacks?," *Focus;* Vol. 2, No. 5 (Joint Center for Political Studies, March 1974), p. 5.

Notes

10. Interview with Alan Baron, Washington, D.C., January 22, 1974.
11. Interview with Bobbie Greene Kilberg, Washington, D.C., January 18, 1974.

CHAPTER 2

1. Phyllis N. Segal, "Women: 2nd Class Democrats," *The New Democrat*, March 1971, pp. 4–5.
2. John S. Saloma III and Frederick H. Sontag, *Parties: The Real Opportunity for Effective Citizen Politics* (New York: Knopf, 1972), p. 109.
3. John M. Blum, Edmund S. Moran, Willie Lee Rose, Arthur M. Schlesinger, Jr., Kenneth M. Stampp, C. Van Woodward, *The National Experience*, 3rd ed. (New York: Harcourt Brace Jovanovich, Inc., 1973), pp. 819–821. This account of the contemporary position of women in American life contains statistics on sex discrimination in other U.S. professions.
4. Mary Costello, "Women Voters," *The Women's Movement: Editorial Research Reports by the Congressional Quarterly* (Washington, D.C.: *Congressional Quarterly*, August 1973), p. 107.
5. Josephine Ripley, "Caucus Blasts," *Christian Science Monitor*, July 27, 1971.
6. Tim O'Brien, "Women's Caucus Seeks U.S. Ban on Sex Bias," Washington *Post*, July 13, 1971; Eileen Shanahan, "Goals Set by Women's Political Caucus," *New York Times*, July 13, 1971.
7. Tim O'Brien, "Women Organize for More Power," Washington *Post*, July 11, 1971.
8. Isabelle Shelton, "Political Caucus Hears Friedan," Washington *Star-News*, July 10, 1971.
9. Interview with Bobbie Greene Kilberg, Washington, D.C., January 18, 1974.
10. Pamela Howard, "Whither the Women's Caucus," *The New Democrat*, October 1971, p. 11.
11. "Women's Group Opens Offensive for Rights Amendment," Washington *Star-News*, August 26, 1971.
12. Isabelle Shelton, "2 Women on Court," Washington *Star-News*, September 24, 1971; "New Women's Caucus Flexes Its Muscle," Washington *Star-News*, September 26, 1971.

Notes

13. Interview with Representative Bella Abzug (New York), Washington, D.C., January 22, 1974.
14. *Ibid.*
15. Interview with Bobbie Greene Kilberg, Washington, D.C., January 18, 1974.
16. Interview with Doris Meissner, former NWPC staff member, Washington, D.C., January 17, 22, 1974.
17. Laurie Lazar, "An Interview with Mrs. Chisholm," *The New Democrat*, November 1971, pp. 8–9.
18. See *Ms.*, Spring 1972; also Isabelle Shelton, "How Dems Stand on Lib," Washington *Sunday Star-News*, March 19, 1972.
19. Deborah Leff, "The Politics of Sex," *The New Democrat*, April 1972, p. 12.
20. There are a number of versions of this incident. See Shirley MacLaine, "Women, the Convention and Brown Paper Bags," *New York Times* Magazine, July 30, 1972; also, Gloria Steinem, "Coming of Age with McGovern: Notes from a Political Diary," *Ms.*, Fall 1972.
21. Steinem, *op cit.*, p. 104.
22. Marsha J. Vandeberg, "Truly a Pioneered Beginning," paper on NWPC prepared for *The New Democrat*, July 18, 1972.
23. Steinem, *op. cit.*, p. 105.
24. Brenda Feigen Fasteau, "What Really Happened with Women in Miami?," *The Village Voice*, July 27, 1972.
25. Steinem, *op. cit.*, p. 103.
26. Fasteau, *op. cit.*
27. See Germaine Greer, "McGovern, the Big Tease," *Harper's*, October 1972; Shana Alexander, *Newsweek*, October 2, 1972; Nora Ephron, "Women," *Esquire*, November 1972.
28. An example of public attacks on McGovern by his own women delegates appears in: Myra MacPherson, "Women Boo as McGovern Skirts their Issues," Washington *Post*, July 11, 1972.
29. Interview with Frank Mankiewicz, Washington, D.C., May 15, 1973.
30. Interviews with Bobbie Greene Kilberg, Washington, D.C., January 18, 1974, and Doris Meissner, Washington, D.C., January 17, 22, 1974.
31. "Shouting Match," United Press International Dispatch, Washington *Star-News*, August 24, 1972.

Notes

32. Jules Witcover, "Sissy Farenthold Is Elected Head of Women's Caucus," Washington *Post*, February 12, 1973.
33. Interview with Representative Bella Abzug (New York), Washington, D.C., January 22, 1974.
34. The Equal Rights Amendment states: "Equality of rights under the law shall not be denied or abridged by the United States or by any state on account of sex."
35. Other women's organizations, which also recruit women interested in politics: National Federation of Business and Professional Women's Clubs, The League of Women Voters, The American Association of University Women; and newer groups: Women's Defense Fund, Women's Lobby, Women's Campaign Fund, Women's Education Fund, Citizen Advisory Council on the Status of Women.
36. Caren Calish, "Interview with Sissy Farenthold," ADA *World*, April–May 1973.
37. "More Women Seeking Public Office this Year in Nation," Hartford *Times*, May 6, 1974.
38. Helen Shaffer, "Status of Women," in *The Women's Movement: Editorial Research Reports by the Congressional Quarterly* (Washington, D.C.: *Congressional Quarterly*, August 1973), p. 57.
39. National Women's Political Caucus, *Fact Sheet*, August 1973.
40. Interview with Jane McMichael, Washington, D.C., January 24, 1974.
41. Quoted in Jules Witcover, "Political Ambitions of American Women Get Watergate Boost," Boston *Evening Globe*, June 20, 1974.
42. "A Mandate To Do What?," *New York Times*, November 10, 1974.

CHAPTER 3

1. *National Roster of Black Elected Officials* (Washington, D.C.: Joint Center for Political Studies, 1974 edition). Nationally, blacks constituted slightly more than one-half of 1 percent of the 522,000 elected officials throughout the country in 1974.
2. *Ibid.*, 1973 edition. As late as 1973, only three blacks had won a statewide office in the entire United States.

Notes

3. "The Black Caucus," *Newsweek*, March 1, 1971, p. 23.
4. "Challenge 1971 Mississippi," *The New Democrat*, January 1971, p. 3.
5. I have drawn heavily for my account of the Mississippi fight on: W. I. Zard, "Congressional Report: The Reform Debacle," *The New Democrat*, February 1971, p. 4; Frank Smith, "How Democrats Screwed Mississippi Liberals," *The New Democrat*, March 1971, pp. 14–15.
6. Howard Romaine, "Why a Black Man Should Run," *The Nation*, September 27, 1971, pp. 264–268.
7. Jude Wanniski, " 'Black Caucus' Gets a White House Surprise," *National Observer*, May 31, 1971.
8. *Ibid.*
9. Eric Wentworth, "Black Calls Nixon Reply 'Charade,' " Washington *Post*, May 23, 1971.
10. Nat Sheppard, "The Congressional Black Caucus in Search of a Role," *Race Relations Reporter*, Vol. 4, March 1973, pp. 18–21.
11. *Ibid.*
12. Channing E. Phillips, "Blacks in the Committee," *The New Democrat*, January 1972, p. 13.
13. "A New Democrat Symposium — What Black Leaders Think of the Democratic Party," *The New Democrat*, May 1971, pp. 3–8.
14. Symposium, *op. cit.*, p. 4.
15. Symposium, *op. cit.*, p. 6.
16. Symposium, *op. cit.*, p. 7.
17. Symposium, *op. cit.*, p. 3.
18. Laurie Lazar, "An Interview with Mrs. Chisholm," *The New Democrat*, November 1971, pp. 8–9.
19. Julian Bond, "The Black Hope," *The New Democrat*, November 1971, p. 7.
20. Samuel Scudder, "Black Caucus Plans National Political Convention," *National Journal*, February 5, 1972.
21. Sheppard, *op. cit.*
22. Paul Delaney, "House Caucus Lists 'Black Bill of Rights,' " *New York Times*, June 1, 1972.
23. The Reverend Jesse Jackson later withdrew his endorsement of Senator McGovern. He was neutral during the presidential campaign.
24. Grayson Mitchell, "Black Politicians' Dream of a National Strategy Fell Apart," Washington *Star-News*, July 5, 1972.

Notes

25. Mitchell, *op. cit.* Note: CBC members were not unanimous about McGovern. Representative Stokes (Ohio) favored Humphrey; Representative Dellums (California) first endorsed Shirley Chisholm, then switched to McGovern.
26. Mitchell, *op. cit.*
27. "The Outsiders on the Inside," *Newsweek*, July 24, 1972.
28. "Black Power Comes of Age," Editorial, Washington *Post*, June 29, 1972.
29. Gary Hart, *Right from the Start* (New York: Quadrangle, 1973), p. 222.
30. Peter Kihss, "Study Analyzes Ethnic Vote in '72," *New York Times*, August 19, 1973. Conclusions from the new epilogue to Mark R. Levy and Michael S. Kramer, *The Ethnic Factor: How America's Minorities Decide Elections*, 2nd ed. (New York City: Simon and Schuster, 1973).
31. William Chapman, "Survey Shows Blacks Loosen Democratic Tie," Washington *Post*, May 5, 1973.
32. Jack Rosenthal, "The 'Secret' Key Issue," *New York Times*, November 5, 1972.
33. Grier Raggio, "Can Liberalism Survive?," *The New Democrat*, April 1970, pp. 2–3.
34. "Black Caucus Drops Role as Minority Spokesman and Emphasizes Legislative Efforts," *New York Times*, May 2, 1973.
35. "Potential Black Voter Influence in CD's," *Focus*; Vol. 1, No. 5 (Joint Center for Political Studies, March 1973), pp. A–D.
36. William Raspberry, "The Fauntroy Memo," Washington *Post*, October 8, 1973.
37. Interview with Augustus A. Adair, Washington, D.C., October 15, 1973.
38. Interview with Robert Maynard, Washington, D.C., November 21, 1973.

CHAPTER 4

1. Damon Stetson, "Meany Sees Democrats Losing Workers' Support," *New York Times*, August 31, 1970.
2. Michael Harrington, "Don't Form a Fourth Party; Form a New First Party," *New York Times* Magazine, September 13, 1970, p. 134.

Notes

3. Jerry Wurf, "What Labor has Against McGovern," *The New Republic*, August 5–12, 1972, pp. 22–23.
4. Harry McPherson, "The Democrats' Dilemma: Watergate Has Undone the Republicans, Right?," *New York Times* Magazine, September 9, 1973, p. 53.
5. Arthur M. Schlesinger, Jr., "The Democrats' Historical Role," *Wall Street Journal*, September 21, 1972.
6. Quoted in David Broder, "Labor Exerting New Muscle in Democratic Party," Washington *Post*, September 2, 1973.
7. Paul Wieck, "Courting Labor," *The New Republic*, September 16, 1972, p. 16.
8. Interview with Bill Lucy, Washington, D.C., August 24, 1973.
9. Paul Wieck, *op. cit.*, p. 16.
10. Interview with Floyd Smith, Washington, D.C., August 27, 1973.
11. Interview with Jerry Wurf, Washington, D.C., September 18, 1973.
12. Interview with Victor Gotbaum, New York City, September 7, 1973.
13. Interview with Joseph Beirne, Washington, D.C., October 2, 1973.
14. Quoted in Ernest R. May and Janet Fraser, eds. *Campaign '72* (Cambridge: Harvard University Press, 1973), 237.
15. Statement of Albert Shanker, President of United Federation of Teachers, submitted to Commission on Delegate Selection and Party Structure of the Democratic National Committee, September 21, 1973.
16. Quoted in David Broder, *op. cit.*
17. Interview with Victor Gotbaum, New York City, September 7, 1973.
18. David Broder, *op. cit.*
19. Interview with David Selden, Washington, D.C., August 16, 1973.
20. Figures cited in "Conference Report," *The Coalition of Black Trade Unionists*, Chicago, Illinois, September 23–24, 1972.
21. "Selected Earnings and Demographic Characteristics of Union Members, 1970," *Report 417, Bureau of Labor Statistics*, U.S. Department of Labor, 1972, p. 1.
22. Paul Delaney, "NAACP Official Doubts Job Gains," *New York Times*, July 4, 1973.
23. Interview with Bill Lucy, Washington, D.C., August 24, 1973.
24. "Ms. Blue Collar," *Time*, May 6, 1974, p. 80.

Notes

25. *Ibid.*
26. Interview with Mildred Jeffrey, Washington, D.C., June 30, 1973.
27. Interview with Joseph Rauh, Jr., Washington, D.C., August 17, 1973.
28. Interview with Msgr. George Higgens, National Catholic Conference, Washington, D.C., August 22, 1973.
29. Interview with Floyd Smith, Washington, D.C., August 27, 1973.
30. Interview with Joseph Rauh, Jr., Washington, D.C., August 17, 1973.
31. For fuller discussion of the UMW and strip-mining, see Peter J. Bernstein, "UMW and Strip Mining: The Curse of Coal," *The Nation*, September 3, 1973, pp. 168–172.

CHAPTER 5

1. "Plan a Reform Push in Party," Kansas City *Times*, November 26, 1968.
2. Interview with Bernard Sorokin, New York City, August 6, 1973.
3. John S. Saloma III and Frederick H. Sontag, *Parties: The Real Opportunity for Effective Citizen Politics* (New York: Knopf, 1972), p. 227.
4. Paul Wieck, "What Happened to the New Politics?," *The New Republic*, February 28, 1970, pp. 12–13.
5. Cited also in Saloma and Sontag, *Parties* p. 226.
6. "The Clean Feeling of Achievement," *The New Republic*, March 14, 1970, pp. 9–11.
7. See David Gelman and Beverly Kempton, "New Issues for the New Politics: An Interview with Richard Goodwin," *The Washington Monthly*, August 1969, pp. 18–19. Goodwin argues that the NDC surrendered its bargaining position by remaining Democratic.
8. Interview with Dan Collins, New York City, November 7, 1973.
9. James Wechsler, "Farewell to Reform," New York *Post*, September 26, 1973.
10. James MacGregor Burns et al., "Can We Save the Party System?," *Schweitzer Humanities Chair Conference*, City University of New York, May 4, 1974.
11. Quoted in Ernest R. May and Janet Fraser, eds, *Campaign '72*

Notes

(Cambridge, Massachusetts: Harvard University Press, 1973), 132–33.

12. Gary Hart, *Right from the Start* (New York: Quadrangle, 1973), p. 75.
13. May and Fraser, *op. cit.*, p. 73.
14. Cited in Richard Dougherty, *Goodbye Mr. Christian: A Personal Account of McGovern's Rise and Fall* (New York: Doubleday, 1973), p. 103.
15. See "A Presidential Caucus," *The New Democrat*, January 1972, p. 23.
16. Richard Dougherty, *op. cit.*, p. 103.
17. Richard H. Miller, "The Mass Caucus Lessons," *The New Democrat*, February 1972, p. 26.
18. William Shannon, "Liberals' Choice — Gene, George or John," *New York Times*, January 23, 1972.
19. Edward Cohen, "A Jumble in Florida," *The New Democrat*, March 1972, p. 22.
20. Hart, *op. cit.*, p. 131.
21. *Ibid.*, p. 149.
22. Thomas Ronan, "McGovern Gains Coalition's Vote," *New York Times*, January 30, 1972.
23. Interview with Richard C. Wade, New York City, September 6, 1973.
24. *Ibid.*
25. Interview with Dan Collins, New York City, November 7, 1973.
26. Interview with Arnold Weiss, New York City, September 4, 1973.
27. Telephone interview with Linda Davidoff, New York City, November 8, 1973.
28. Michael Kenney and Peter Lucas, "McGovern Activists Desert, Regulars Control Mass. Party," Boston *Sunday Globe*, May 26, 1974.

CHAPTER 6

1. Mike Duberstein, "Washington Report — A BAS Seniority," *The New Democrat*, April 1970, pp. 4–5.
2. *Ibid.*

Notes

3. Interview with Richard Conlon, Washington, D.C., April 20, 30, and May 2, 1973.
4. Interview with Representative James O'Hara (Michigan), Washington, D.C., May 9, 1973.
5. Interview with Richard Conlon, Washington, D.C., April 20, 30, and May 2, 1973.
6. Interview with Representative James O'Hara (Michigan), Washington, D.C., May 9, 1973.
7. "The First Year of Record Teller Voting," *Democratic Study Group Special Report*, January 27, 1972.
8. Mike Duberstein, "Congressional Report: The Reform Debacle," *The New Democrat*, February 1971, p. 4.
9. Mike Duberstein, "Congressional Watch: Vietnam Postponed," *The New Democrat*, April 1971, p. 2.
10. Interview with Representative Phillip Burton (California), Washington, D.C., April 30, 1973. Burton was only technically accurate in his reference to 92 DSG members prior to his election as chairman. Actually, there were about 140, but 40 to 50 had not paid their dues in 1970 though they continued to attend meetings and receive mailings.
11. Mike Duberstein, "Congressional Watch: Vietnam Postponed," *The New Democrat*, April 1971, p. 2; "Congressional Watch: The Dellums Hearings," *The New Democrat*, June 1971, p. 5; "Congressional Watch: The Democratic Freeze, *The New Democrat*, December 1971, p. 14; "Congressional Watch: House Election '72," *The New Democrat*, March 1972, p. 18; "Congressional Watch: Silent Revolution in the House," *The New Democrat*, Summer 1972, p. 44.
12. Interview with Richard Conlon, Washington, D.C., April 20, 30 and May 2, 1973.
13. *Ibid.*
14. Interview with David Broder, Washington, D.C., April 25, 1973.
15. *Ibid.*
16. Interview with Representative John Culver (Iowa), Washington, D.C., May 16, 1973.
17. Interview with Democratic Majority Leader Thomas P. O'Neill, Jr. (Massachusetts), Washington, D.C., May 17, 1973.
18. Representative Robert Drinan (Massachusetts), "Pretending Reform," *The Nation*, February 12, 1973, p. 196.

Notes

19. Interview with Representative Richard Bolling (Missouri), Washington, D.C., May 7, 1973.
20. Interview with Richard Conlon, Washington, D.C., April 20, 30, and May 2, 1973.
21. Albert Hunt, "How the Democrats Bungled the Price Rollback," *The Wall Street Journal*, April 23, 1973.
22. Interview with Richard Conlon, Washington, D.C., April 20, 30, and May 2, 1973.
23. Interview with Democratic Majority Leader Thomas P. O'Neill, Jr. (Massachusetts), Washington, D.C., May 17, 1973.
24. *Ibid.*
25. Interview with Representative Donald Fraser (Minnesota), Washington, D.C., April 20, 1973.

CHAPTER 7

1. Paul Wieck, "Fiesta at Espanola: Doubts About McGovern," *The New Republic*, September 23, 1972, p. 14.
2. Wieck, *op. cit.*, p. 15.
3. Wieck, *op. cit.*, p. 13.
4. Senator Joseph Montoya, "Woe Unto Those Who Have Ears But Do Not Hear," *The Congressional Record*, May 16, 1971, S6314.
5. For further history on the Crystal City upheaval, see Peter Barnes, "Chicano Power: Liberating a County," *The New Republic*, December 1, 1973.
6. Wieck, *op. cit.*, p. 14.
7. These figures are taken from Mark R. Levy and Michael S. Kramer, *The Ethnic Factor: How America's Minorities Decide Elections*, 2nd ed. (New York City: Simon & Schuster, 1973).
8. Representative Herman Badillo (New York), "The Today Show," National Broadcasting Company, April 3, 1974.
9. *Ibid.*
10. James P. Sterba, "Indian Militants Appeal for Unity," *New York Times*, October 31, 1973.
11. Legislative Alert, No. 16, *Native American Lobby*, May–June 1972.
12. *Ibid.*
13. Wieck, *op. cit.*, p. 15.

Notes

14. *Ibid.*
15. Martin Waldron, "U.S. Indians Press Drive to Get Independent Status," *New York Times,* August 19, 1974.
16. Testimony of Ernest O. Reaugh, National Coalition of Gay Organizations, before the Democratic National Platform Committee Hearings, Boston, Mass., May 30, 1972.
17. Theodore White, *The Making of the President* 1972 (New York City: Bantam Books, 1973), p. 239.
18. Arthur Bell, "Has the Gay Movement Gone Establishment?," *The Village Voice,* March 28, 1974, p. 16.
19. *Ibid.*
20. Judith Cummings, "Homosexual-Rights Law Shows Progress In Some Cities, But Drive Arouses Considerable Opposition," *New York Times,* May 13, 1974.

CHAPTER 8

1. Roper Poll, September 1974, cited in *Time,* October 14, 1974, p. 13.
2. Herbert Alexander, *Financing the 1968 Election* (Lexington, Massachusetts: D. C. Heath and Co., 1971), p. 30.
3. *Ibid.,* p. 10.
4. Interview with Herbert Alexander, New York City, May 30, 1973.
5. Alexander, *Financing the 1968 Election, op. cit.,* p. 30.
6. Interview with Jeff Smith, Washington, D.C., May 15, 1973.
7. Interview with Frank Mankiewicz, Washington, D.C., May 15, 1973.
8. Interview with Jeff Smith, Washington, D.C., May 15, 1973.
9. Ted Van Dyk, "The Hero of A Year Ago," *The Washington Monthly,* May 1973, pp. 40–41.
10. Dr. Clifford Brown, Jr., "The Gap in GOP Campaign Funds," *Wall Street Journal,* May 28, 1974.
11. Brown, *op. cit.*
12. Arthur H. Miller, Warren E. Miller, Alden S. Raine, Thad A. Brown, "A Majority Party in Disarray: Policy Polarization in the 1972 Election," the University of Michigan Center for Political Studies, prepared for the American Political Science Association, September 4–8, 1973, New Orleans, Louisiana.

Notes

13. *Ibid.*, p. 13.
14. *Ibid.*, p. 12.
15. *Ibid.*, p. 71.
16. Louis Harris, *The Anguish of Change* (New York: W. W. Norton, 1973), p. 273.
17. Eileen Shanahan, "Income Distribution Found Unchanged," *New York Times*, February 1, 1974. Figures are drawn from the President's Annual Economic Report, prepared by the Council of Economic Advisors for 1973.
18. Morton Mintz, "8 Institutions Control Most of Top Firms," *Washington Post*, January 6, 1973.
19. James L. Rowe, Jr., "Big Firms Escape Taxes, Study Says," *Washington Post*, December 19, 1974.
20. Alice M. Rivlin, "Why Should Liberals Bleed When the President Cuts? A Counter-Budget for Social Progress," *New York Times* Magazine, April 8, 1973, p. 86.
21. Samuel Lubell, *The Hidden Crisis in American Politics* (New York: W. W. Norton & Co., 1970), p. 87.
22. Quoted in Tom Wicker, "Ted & Geo & Dick & Strom," *New York Times*, July 6, 1973.
23. John Kenneth Galbraith, *Economics and the Public Purpose* (Boston: Houghton Mifflin Co., 1973).
24. Interview with Michael Harrington, New York City, March 2, 1973.
25. "We Are Socialists of the Democratic Left, Founding Statement," Democratic Socialist Organizing Committee, New York City, October 12, 1973.
26. Quote by Joseph Rauh, Jr., at ad hoc meeting of liberals, New York City, December 16, 1972.
27. Tom Wicker, "An Army Without a General," *New York Times*, March 24, 1974.
28. J. W. Anderson, "Public Indifference? On the Watergate and the Returns," *Washington Post*, November 9, 1972.

Index

Abel, I. W., 2

Abzug, Bella: and NWPC, 12, 27, 29, 48; on prejudice against women, 28–29; her ideological split with Betty Friedan, 28–29, 44, 51; and delegate selection, 32–33; and Shirley Chisholm's presidential candidacy, 35, 36; feminist program presented to Democratic Platform Committee by, 37; and 1972 Democratic Convention, 39; on the NDCs, 135

ADA, *see* Americans for Democratic Action

Adair, Augustus Alven, 78

AFL-CIO, 11, 67, 77, 103, 107; position of, on the issues, 82, 86–87; UAW departure from, 83; Michael Harrington on, 86; and union split over McGovern, 88, 90–98 *passim*, 199; black membership in, 102

AFSCME, *see* American Federation of State, County and Municipal Employees

Albert, Carl, 4, 159; and the CBC, 53; and Conyers, 55; and the DSG, 148, 149, 150; conversion of, to reform, 154

Alexander, Shana, 42

Amalgamated Meatcutters, 92, 96

American Association of University Women, 27

American Federation of State, County and Municipal Employees (AFSCME), 87, 92, 93, 94–95, 98; progressiveness of, 84, 96; black membership of, 102

American Federation of Teachers (AFT), 96

American Indian Movement (AIM), 180–81

Americans For Democratic Action (ADA), 98, 109, 119, 127, 162; contribution of labor to, 81; 1968 endorsement of McCarthy by, 82, 97; function of, 110; reliability of, compared with NDC, 111–12; and NDC, 134; strength of, 135

Anderson, J. W., 213

Armstrong, Anne, 29

Ashbrook, John, 35

Badillo, Herman, 117, 174, 177–78, 179

Baraka, Imamu (LeRoi Jones), 67

Barkan, Alexander E., 82, 90, 98–99, 100, 101, 108

Baron, Alan, 22

Bayh, Birch, 97

Beame, Abe, 117, 177

Beirne, Joseph, 84, 95–96, 97, 100, 101

Bell, Arthur, 190

Bentley, Helen, 29, 30

Index

Index

Index

Friedan, Betty: *The Feminine Mystique,* 24; and NWPC, 27, 28, 29; and NOW, 28; her ideological split with Bella Abzug, 28–29, 44, 51; and debate over Chisholm and McGovern, 36; volatile nature of, 41; appearance of, at Republican Convention, 44

Galbraith, John Kenneth, 206–8, 209
Gary convention, *see* National Black Political Convention
Gay Activists Alliance (GAA), 185, 186, 190, 191
Gays, 165, 192; entrance of, into public consciousness, 184–85; efforts to end discrimination against, 185–87, 191; and 1972 Democratic Convention, 187–89, crumbling of their movement, 190
Gibson, Ken, 71, 79
Goldman, Mari, 49
Goldwater, Barry, 4, 55, 140–41, 184, 195
Goodell, Charles, 197
Gorman, Patrick, 96
Gotbaum, Victor, 95, 99
Graphic Arts Union, 93, 98
Gravel, Mike, 41
Green, Edith, 25
Greene, Don, 111
Greer, Germaine, 42
Grospiron, Al, 96
Grossman, Jerome, 121, 135
Guggenheimer, Elinor, 191
Gutierrez, José Angel, 171–72
Gwirtzman, Milt, 166

Hamer, Fannie Lou, 57
Hansen, Julia Butler, 145, 147, 152, 154
Harper's, 42
Harrington, Michael, 86, 208–9
Harris, Fred, 128, 183
Harris, La Donna, 183
Harris, Louis, 192, 202–3
Harris, Patricia, 82

Hart, Gary, 40, 71–72, 120–21, 123, 124
Hartke, Vance, 35
Hatcher, Richard, 62, 67, 79
Hatfield, Mark, 197
Hauser, Rita, 30
Haynsworth, Clement, 53
Heckler, Margaret, 43
Henry, Aaron, 53–54, 56
Hernandez-Colon, Rafael, 175–77
Holifield, Chet, 151
Hotel and Restaurant Employees Union, 104
Howard, Pamela, 30–31
Hughes, Harold, 82, 197
Humphrey, Hubert H., 68, 123, 126, 189, 201; and 1968 Democratic Convention, 1, 2; his ties with labor, 11, 88, 124; and discrimination against women in politics, 26; and NWPC, 37; and civil rights, 57; black vote for (1968), 73; and election of 1968; 74; 1968 nomination of, 82; and COPE, 95; and the GAA, 186; and the three A's, 188; fund-raising for campaign of, 195; defeated by McGovern in California, 199
Humphreys, Laud, 186
Hunt, Albert, 160

Ickes, Harold, Jr., 110
Indian Affairs, Bureau of, 179, 180
Indian Affairs, Office of, proposed, 182
Indians, 165, 192; awakening of consciousness among, 179–80; organizations of, 180–81; recognition of, by political leaders, 181–83; relations between Chicanos and, 183; possibility of political movement among, 183–84
International Association of Machinists (IAM), 84, 92, 93, 94, 98
International Union of Electricians, 93

233

Index

Jackson, Eleanor, 5
Jackson, Henry, 2, 14, 35, 88, 95, 188
Jackson, Jesse, 68, 71, 73, 78
Jeffrey, Mildred, 104
Johnson, Lyndon B., 58, 83, 88, 195; and 1968 Democratic Convention, 1; rebellion of liberals against, 109; and the DSG, 141
Jordan, Vernon, 206

Keefe, Robert, 90, 97
Kennedy, Edward M., 122
Kennedy, John F., 141
Kennedy, Robert F., 74–75, 86, 121, 206; and 1968 Democratic Convention, 1, 2; vision of, 79; campaign of, 82, 109–10; union support for, 85; and Marco Rigau, Jr., 175; interest of, in the Indians, 181; fund-raising for campaign of, 194–95, 196; and Jeff Smith, 197
Kilberg, Bobbie Greene, 19–20, 22–23, 29, 33
King, Coretta, 62, 68
Kinsey, Alfred, 186–87
Kirkland, Lane, 89
Kramer, Michael, 111

Laird, Melvin, 53
Lazar, Laurie, 5, 34
League of Women Voters, 34
Leff, Deborah, 36
Lehman, Herbert, 118
Lindsay, John, 121, 124, 125, 127; George Meany on, 88; and NDC, 116; and Massachusetts caucus, 122, 123; GAA heckling of, 185
Lowenstein, Allard, 191
Lubell, Samuel, 79, 205
Lucy, Bill, 93

McCarthy, Eugene, 57–58, 125, 127, 128; and 1968 Democratic Convention, 1, 2; campaign of, 82, 109–10; ADA endorsement of, 97; and the NDC Massachusetts caucus, 122, 123; and DSG, 140; fund-

raising for campaign of, 194–95, 196
McCormack, John, 4, 141, 142
McGee, Gale, 114
McGovern, George, 11, 82, 83, 207; nomination of, 5, 45–46; his removal of Lawrence O'Brien, 8; defeat of, 14, 47, 73; and NWPC, 36, 37; on issue of abortion, 38, 40, 41; and 1972 Democratic Convention, 39–43; CBC's support for, 68–73; defeat of, attributable to race issue, 73–74; Meany's opposition to, 87–91; union split over, 91–99, 108; and NDC, 114, 119, 120–27, 128, 129–33; and the Chicanos, 166–70, 172–73; and Marco Rigau, 175; and Herman Badillo, 177; Indian program of, 181–83; and the Gay movement, 186, 187–90; fund-raising for campaign of, 195–200; Michigan study on campaign of, 201–2; weakness of, in 1972, 203; Tom Wicker on, 212. *See also* McGovern-Fraser Commission on Party Structure and Delegate Selection
McGovern-Fraser Commission on Party Structure and Delegate Selection, 8, 9, 19, 20, 84; formation of, 1, 2; guidelines of, 3, 6–7; underrepresentation of women on, 25; Meany's ordering of COPE to boycott, 82
McKay, Martha, 41
MacLaine, Shirley, 37, 38
McMichael, Jane, 50
Maddox, Lester, 2
Madeson, Marvin, 113, 114
Mankiewicz, Frank, 43, 198
Mansfield, Mike, 4, 148
Martin, Yancy, 71
Massachusetts Citizens for Participation in Politics (CPP), 121
Massachusetts Political Action for Peace (Mass PAX), 114–15, 121
Maynard, Robert, 78–79

Index

Meany, George, 11, 14, 84, 85, 106, 107; position of, on the issues, 82–83, 87; Michael Harrington on, 86; his hostility toward McGovern, 87–91; and 1972 Democratic Convention, 90; challenge to, 94, 95, 96, 108; and Nixon, 101; and CBTU, 102–3; and CLUW, 104

Merrill, Rick, 137–38

Mexican-American Political Association (MAPA), 173

Mikulski, Barbara, her Commission on Delegate Selection, 15, 46, 99, 100

Miller, Arnold, 98, 105, 106–7

Million Member Club, 199

Mills, Wilbur, 35

Mississippi Freedom Democratic Party, 57

Mississippi Loyalist Democratic Party, 53–55, 57

Mitchell, Parran J., 64

Mixner, David, 110

Montoya, Joseph, 168, 169–70, 171

Mott, Stewart, 38–39, 154

Ms., 35, 37

Muñoz, Marín, Luis, 175–76

Murphy, John, 151

Muskie, Edmund, 37, 59, 87, 121, 124, 128; and NDC Massachusetts caucus, 122, 123

NAACP, 12

Nation, The, 157

National Black Political Convention (Gary, Indiana), 67–68, 69, 73

National Coalition of Gay Organizations, 185–87

National Committee for an Effective Congress (NCEC), 109, 112

National Congress of American Indians (NCAI), 180

National Council for a Liveable World, 109

National Education Association (NEA), 91, 92, 107

National Gay Task Force, 190–91

National GI Forum, 173

National League of Cities, 77

National Maritime Union, 105, 106

National Organization for Women (NOW), 11–12; emergence of, 24; and NWPC, 28, 31, 48

National Treasury Employees Union, 92

National Tribal Chairman's Association (NTCA), 180

National Welfare Rights Organization (NWRO), 113

National Women's Political Caucus (NWPC), 12, 17, 18, 19; creation and impact of, 27; goals of, 27–28, 36; differences within, 28–29; growth of, 29–30; Pamela Howard on, 30–31; and delegate selection, 31–34, 35; and Bella Abzug, 32; and presidential politics, 34–36; failure of, to endorse Chisholm's presidential candidacy, 35, 66; program of, presented to Democratic Platform Committee meeting, 37–38; on issue of abortion, 38, 40–41, 42, 43, 44, 50; and 1972 Democratic Convention, 38–43; vice-presidency fight of, 41, 42; criticisms of, 42; and 1972 Republican Convention, 43–45; Houston Conference of, 46–48; political activities of, since 1972, 48–51; and CLUW, 104

National Youth Caucus, 11, 121

Native American Lobby, 181

NCEC, *see* National Committee for an Effective Congress

NDC, *see* New Democratic Coalition

NEA, *see* National Education Association

New Democrat, The, 10, 37; formation of, 4–5; on Democratic Party reforms, 6–8, 82; on discrimination against women in politics, 24, 25–26; and NWPC, 27, 30, 34, 36, 38–39; and controversy over seating of five Mississippi congressmen, 53–56, 58; and the CBC, 61; on "Black Caucusing," 62; symposium

235

Index

Index

Index

Wade, Richard C., 125–26, 132–33, 134
Waldron, Martin, 184
Wall Street Journal, 160, 199
Wallace, George, 79, 126, 189, 201; large movement behind, 16, 194; and proportional representational system, 17; and NWPC, 35, 38; and election of 1968, 74; his address to Southern Conference of Black Mayors, 77; and delegate selection, 200
Walters, Donald, 21–22
Washington Monthly, The, 199
Washington *Post,* 127, 153, 204, 213; on CBC-McGovern pact, 70; on black movements, 78; on COPE, 99
Watergate scandals, 75, 77
Watts, Glenn E., 97
Wechsler, James, 118
WEDS, *see* Women's Education for Delegate Selection
Weiss, Arnold, 133–34
Westwood, Jean, 8, 46, 99
White, Theodore, 188

Wicker, Tom, 212
Wieck, Paul, 91–92, 94; on the NDC, 114; on McGovern's Chicano policy, 168–70; on La Raza Unida, 172; on growth of Indian political awareness, 182; on relations between Chicanos and Indians, 183
Wiley, George, 113
Willkie, Wendell, 211
Williams, John Bell, 55
Wolfgang, Myra, 103–4
Women's Christian Temperance Union, 31
Women's Education For Delegate Selection (WEDS), 12, 34
Women's Strike for Peace, 27
Woodcock, Leonard, 87, 104
Wurf, Jerry, 87, 88–89, 94–95, 96, 101, 106

Yankelovich, Daniel, 73–74
Yorty, Sam, 35

Zablocki, Clement, 151